Home Centered Care

Designing a Family Day Care Program

A Guide For Caregivers and Parents

by Ronda Garcia

Edited by Lenore Thompson
and Marian McDonald

Illustrated by Linda Revel
Photographed by Angelika I. Wagner-Garrett

gryphon house
Mt. Rainier, Maryland

Preparation for the first edition of this book was made possible
by a grant from The San Francisco Foundation.

Interior design by Linda Revel
Cover design by Graves Fowler Associates
Cover photograph by John Burwell

Second Edition–1986
Third Edition–1991

Published by Gryphon House, Inc., P.O. Box 275, Mt. Rainier, MD 20712

Library of Congress Catalog Card Number: 91-71103

ISBN 0-87659-154-3

Publisher's Cataloging in Publication
(Prepared by Quality Books Inc.)

Garcia, Ronda.
Home centered care : designing a family day care program : a guide for caregivers and parents / by Ronda Garcia. --
p. cm.
Includes bibliographical references and index.
ISBN 0-87659-154-3

1. Family day care--United States. 2. Child development--United States. I. Title.

HV854 649'.1
QBI91-548

TABLE OF CONTENTS

ACKNOWLEDGMENTS

This book represents years of work by many people. It was compiled by parents and caregivers throughout San Francisco's neighborhoods. It was critiqued and edited by early childhood education specialists. It was funded by the San Francisco Foundation, and supported by my family, friends and colleagues. It represents a decade of playing with and observing babies and toddlers. It represents years of watching them grow to adolescence and adulthood. And this is my opportunity to thank all of you who have shared your knowledge, your insights and your love.

Christina Cuevas at the San Francisco Foundation has advocated for continued funding of the Family Day Care Recruitment and Training Project. Based in low-income neighborhoods, this project worked with community agencies to train and improve the quality of childcare in our multi-ethnic, urban setting.

As project coordinator, I had the opportunity to work with hundreds of caregivers throughout the city. Their feedback and critique of my work is the very foundation of this book. They shared their experiences, stories, frustrations and dreams. They taught me that family day care is more than a job. So thank you Mrs. Brown, Mary, Lillian, Raquel, Aileen, Judith, Mrs. Evans, Graciella, Cuca, Juanita and Betty.

Santiago Ruiz, Executive Director at Mission Neighborhood Centers, Joseph Crafton, Executive Director at Audrey L. Smith Developmental Centers, Inc. and Martha Roditti, Executive Director at the Children's Council of San Francisco, directed and supported the collaborative spirit of the training project. Their insights and expertise allowed us to execute a successful and effective training.

My supervisor and co-workers at The Children's Council of San Francisco supported and encouraged the completion of this manuscript. Thank you Marian McDonald (editor), Linda Revel (artist and production), Ufahamu Kent (Family Day Care Specialist), Deborah Morrison (multi-cultural contributor), Ana Sainten (activities contributor), Andrew Scott (technical assistance), Pwekedia Williams (last minute emergencies), and Martha Roditti for her trust and faith in my capabilities.

Books are written because someone sits down day after day and writes and rewrites until the job is done. This book would not have been completed without the persuasion (and nagging) of some exceptional people. Lenore Thompson was my most inspiring supporter and staunchest critic. We worked together on a regular basis as we questioned and refined theorectical knowledge into practical and concise language. My editor, Marian McDonald, understood the importance of seeing this project through to completion, and labored with me over the details. Harre Demoro and Shari Weissman read the copy in its early stages and Paul Boden proofed the final manuscript.

My husband, Reg Garcia, offered his love and support.

A gracious thank you to Janet Gonzalez-Mena and the faculty at Pacific Oaks College, who read the manuscript in the beginning stages, and my mother Shirl Hutton who was there at the end (she claims she was there in the beginning too).

For all those children whose diapers I've changed and noses I've wiped, I thank you for your laughter, your tears and your hugs. I thought of you. Sasha and Kayla and Ali and Daniel, as I wrote about children playing and growing. I thought of you, Rebecca and Dylan and Jesse, as I wrote about babies who reached for their dreams.

And for my own children, Kayce and David, who taught me that caring and giving are really one word.

INTRODUCTION

The idea of writing a book for caregivers is something I have been thinking about for a long time. As a professional working in early childhood education programs I was struck with how much we know about children, and how little of that we write down to be shared. We tend to keep our tricks to ourselves, knowing that what works with one child doesn't necessarily work with another.

This book is the writing down of some of those tricks. They were taught to me by people, like many of you, who have been working with children for a very long time. As parents and professional caregivers, you have shared the joys and challenges of helping children become all that they are meant to be. You have talked to me about the many ways that children reveal their charisma and magic.

No person can better teach about ways to bring out the best in children than my first teacher, Magda Gerber. She has a special knack for communicating the essentials of what children need from us as adult caregivers. She teaches the principle of relating to young children with respect. By treating children with respect we allow their sense of self-worth to develop, and at the same time create respectful environments for ourselves. By investing in their growth, we are also investing in our own.

Another element of Mrs. Gerber's philosophy is the importance of weaving consistency and predictability into the fabric of a children's daily life. In order to thrive, children need the people caring for them to be predictable and consistent from day to day.

This book is essentially my interpretation of her teachings. It is a practical and realistic guide to putting theory into everyday practice. The book is designed to give a consistent approach to child development and caregiving concepts. Because of this consistency you can read the book from beginning to end, or from the middle outward, and still have an understanding of what children need. Whether in a description of an art activity or an outline of the developmental needs and likes of toddlers, this book offers a consistent guide to applying sound caregiving concepts.

There are no special chapters for children with "special needs" or for non-sexist play. Each word in this book approaches all children as special, with their own personal pace for growing and learning. It is respectful of children's limitations as well as their competencies.

The book recognizes the need for women and girls to be portrayed in literature as powerful and active. The use of female pronouns is used primarily to describe situations when children are active and engaged in challenging play.

Caregivers is a professional term which is applicable to both sexes, and emphasizes the caring aspect more than the teaching aspect of being with young children. I use "parent" and "parent(s)" interchangeably to convey both the traditional, as well as the unconventional, families and lifestyles which make this world a diverse place to live.

Discrimination is a very real part of the childcaring profession. As caregivers we have the opportunity either to perpetuate an intolerant system, or to begin to make a difference. We can choose to integrate our homes, our schools and our community by offering all families access to affordable, quality programs.

Section I

DESIGNING PHYSICALLY SAFE ENVIRONMENTS FOR CHILDREN

HOME is many things to many people. For most of us, home is a place of warmth and security, a rest from an often hectic world. For the children in your care, your home is also one of their first places of learning.

We know that from the youngest age, children are learning through their daily experiences with their family, their caregivers and their surroundings. This section will help you plan a safe and nurturing environment for the children in your home.

Chapter 1

FOR EXPLORATION AND LEARNING

The way you arrange your home, both indoors and out, influences what children will learn. As caregivers you are responsible for the day to day caring of young children. Your home, regardless of size, can provide a setting which is both inviting and safe.

By creating safe environments for children, you make it possible for them to feel calm and comfortable in your home. These feelings encourage children to explore and learn new things.

Feelings of safety and security are particularly important to young children in child care. Before opening your family day care home, there are basic precautions required for licensing in your state, like putting a gate across the stairs and covering the electrical outlets. You will be designing a place for the children to play with their toys, crawl around the room and have a good time with each other.

The following chapters will help you to determine some ways to create play areas in your home which are appropriate for the different ages and needs of the children in your care. These areas may include the kitchen, the living room or any combination of rooms in your home.

First, decide which areas can be used by the children without your constant supervision. This is important because many times during the day you will be called to different parts of your home to prepare food, answer the telephone, wash hands, change diapers or check a sleeping child. It is impossible to be everywhere at once. You must limit how much you expect yourself to supervise. No one can watch the basement and attic at the same time. Realizing this can make your job easier.

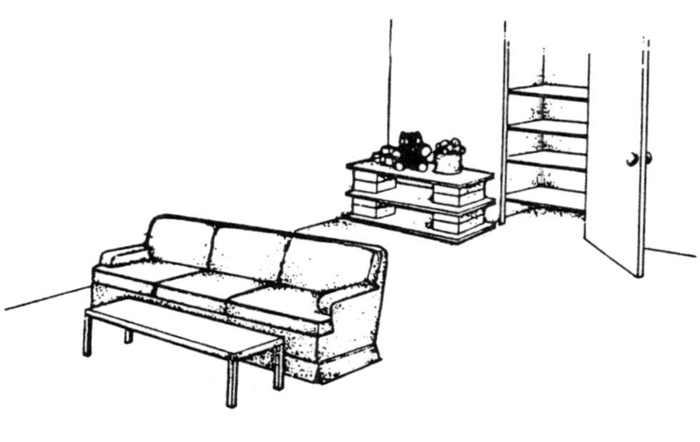

When designing an environment for exploration and learning it is important that you look at each room and the ways you can adopt them to areas for play.

To begin, it is necessary to first look at safety factors and decide which parts of the house children can use during different times of the day. They will need places to eat, sleep, play with their toys and be with each other.

Everything in a child's environment communicates how the child should behave in that setting. Thus it is helpful to try to look at the environment from the child's point of view.

There are many ways to design a home environment for children without completely restructuring your entire living space and spending a lot of money. How you decide to arrange the furniture, display the toys, create storage areas, arrange for active play outside, and store personal belongings are important considerations.

1. First, decide which rooms will be most heavily used for children's activities. You do have choices. The kitchen may be an ideal place for messy art activities because it is close to water and the floor can be easily cleaned.

The living room/dining room may be more spacious if the furniture is moved back and sections are provided for children's toys and materials. An extra bedroom or family room may also be well suited for some activities.

2. Remember, the arrangement of each room will depend on the size of your home or apartment, the number of people in your household, and the size and the age range of the children you are caring for.

3. Decide how you want to organize these rooms in order to encourage the children's exploration of play materials.

4. If your license permits you to care for children under 2 years of age, you will already have cribs for sleeping, a sanitary diaper changing area, and adequate space for them to move freely.

5. For preschool and school-age children, you will need spaces for active play, table tops for drawing, table games, puzzles and homework. Boys and girls also require areas for building, playing house, and reading stories.

Chapter 2
ARRANGING YOUR FAMILY DAY CARE HOME

LIVING ROOM, DINING ROOM OR FAMILY ROOM:

This may be where you and the children will spend the majority of time during the day. Doing a good job of arranging this room will make supervision easier.

- Use furniture already in the room to create boundaries for play. Your existing couches and bookcases can become partitions for quiet and active play materials.
- Use nonslip area rugs to help define play spaces. Add pillows and a basket of books for a quiet reading area or a soft place to watch television.
- Think about using your tables as places where the children might draw pictures, play board games, or do homework.
- Use shelves to make toys accessible. Clear the existing shelves in the room which are within eye level and a child's reach. Build inexpensive shelves, or make shelves by using sturdy cartons from the grocery store. Some caregivers use empty ice cream containers to create additional display spaces for toys or storage of personal belongings.
- The children's play area should be well lighted and ventilated.
  - Windows should be double checked for safety, so children cannot fall out of the building.
- Select which toys you will put out each day.
  - Remember that children need to have the same selection of toys available from day to day, to give them a sense of security. These will vary depending on which are the most liked and suitable for their development at the time. But too many toys will be distracting and a chore to pick up. **Many caregivers rotate their family day care toys so that not everything is available at once, and so they have something "new" to take out at different times.**

KITCHEN: This is usually the room you will be using for meal preparation and where the children will be eating.

- A low table and chairs (or booster seats on the floor) are ideal for children. They should be able to seat themselves so their feet touch the floor.

- If a low table is not available, be sure that the children can sit safely at the table.

- Handwashing is a key to the prevention of illness. Have a step stool ready so the children can wash their own hands before and after meals.

The kitchen is often the best place for messy activities.

- Use an oil cloth, old shower curtain, or canvas tarp to protect your floor.

- Being close to the kitchen sink will make cleanup easier. The children should be encouraged to help.

- Water play activities with soapy bubbles or toys which float can be just as successful in one inch of water as with four inches in a plastic tub or dishpan. And there will be much less of a mess.

BEDROOM AND BATHROOM: These rooms are often used by the children for naps, diapering and toileting. Because children are sometimes in these rooms unsupervised, it is important that you take particular precautions to keep detergents, cleansers, medicines and perfumes out of reach.

- Cribs, beds, cots and mattresses can be used for naps. Try to give children the same place to nap each day. This consistency will make it easier for the child to rest and fall asleep.

- Diaper changing areas should have access to water. Many caregivers find it helpful to set up the diapering area each day with everything they will need right at their fingertips. This way when it is time to diaper the baby, the caregiver will not be distracted trying to find things and will have time to focus on the diapering. Remember that children learn from their experiences, and diapering is one experience which happens approximately 7,000 times during the first three years. Try to make this time enjoyable for the child. The caregiver should be sure to wash his hands after diapering.

You will be surprised at how cooperative young babies can be when they are involved in the diapering process.

Try not to distract them with toys and mobiles. Instead focus on communicating what the baby is experiencing and learning. Refer to Section III, for some practical applications of how to involve infants in everyday situations.

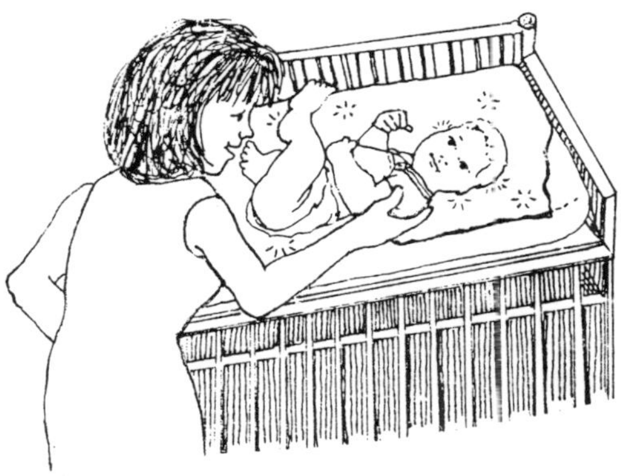

"I will take off this wet diaper. Can you help me by lifting your legs?"

- Unused rooms in your family day care home should be latched with a large hook and eye. You can buy these at most hardware stores.

- Garage and basement areas which are not used by children should be kept locked at all times.

If children pass through these areas to get outside, passage ways should be kept clutter free. Keep dangerous chemicals, poisons and sharp tools in locked cabinets. Using basement and garage areas for caring for young children is becoming increasingly more common. Be sure to follow common sense health and safety guidelines, and pay particular attention to ventilation, lighting and heating.

REFERENCES

Gerber, M. *Resources for Infant Educarers*. Los Angeles, CA: 1550 Murray Circle 90026. 1981.

——————— "What is Appropriate Curriculum for Infants and Toddlers?", in Weissbound B. and Musick J., ed., *Infants: Their Social Environments.* Washington, D.C.: National Association for the Education of Young Children, 1981.

Fish, D. *Home Based Training Resource Handbook.* Toys 'n Things Training & Resource Center, Inc., St. Paul, Minn. 1980.

Frank L. In "Introduction" to Hartley R. and Goldenson, R. *The Complete Book of Children's Play.* New York: Thomas Crowell, 1970.

Hymes, J. *Teaching the Child Under Six.* Columbus, Ohio: Charles E. Merrill and Company, 1979.

Kritchensky, S. and Prescott L. *Planning Environments for Young Children: Physical Space*. Washington, D.C.: National Association for the Education of Young Children, 1969.

Pikler, E. "Some Contributions to the Study of the Gross Motor Development of Children," *Journal of Genetic Psychology,* Vol. 113 (1968): 27-39.

Stone, J. and Rodolph, N. *Play and Playgrounds*. Washington, D.C.: National Association for the Education of Young Children, 1969.

Sunset Books, *Sunset Ideas for Children's Rooms and Play Yards* Menlo Park, CA: Lane Publishing Co., 1979.

Section II

GROWING UP —— CHILDREN'S DEVELOPING LIKES AND NEEDS

THE VERY YOUNG CHILD is in a continuous process of growth and change. This section on child development will discuss the stages during which many normal child behavior patterns develop. Knowledge of these growth stages can help you know what to expect, what age you may expect specific problems to occur, and how you can help at each developmental age and stage.

This section has been formatted to give you detailed insight into how the likes and needs of children emerge. Understanding what children like at different developmental stages will enable you to better respond to their needs.

Each chapter addresses children's physical, social and emotional likes and what they need from you. In Chapter 3 you will read about what infants like and what they need at this age. You will discover that your ability to respond sensitively to physical, social and emotional likes is the key to treating children with respect.

Chapters 4, 5 and 6 detail the likes and needs of toddler through school-age children from this same developmental perspective.

The way you react to children's needs will influence how they grow. Caring for young children with respect is more than being nice to them. It requires a partnership between the children's ability to communicate their likes, and your ability to interpret into action what they need from you.

Chapter 3

INFANT DEVELOPMENT

What Do Infants (0 to 15 months) Like?

PHYSICAL:

- INFANTS LIKE to feel safe where they are placed.
- INFANTS LIKE to explore their hands and toes.
- INFANTS LIKE to be close to your body.
- INFANTS LIKE to be held close enough to see your familiar face.
- INFANTS LIKE to have familiar objects to explore with their mouths and their hands.
- INFANTS LIKE to know that if they cry when they are hungry, food will be available.
- INFANTS LIKE to be checked for a wet diaper.

SOCIAL:

- INFANTS LIKE to be placed close to you and others.
- INFANTS LIKE to be talked to.
- INFANTS LIKE to be put in positions where they can watch you and other children.
- INFANTS LIKE to be sung to...even if they are not sleepy.
- INFANTS LIKE when you talk to them while you are feeding and when you are diapering them.

EMOTIONAL:

- INFANTS LIKE to be soothed when they fuss.
- INFANTS LIKE you to smile at them.
- INFANTS LIKE to be comforted and held when they are upset and become frightened.
- INFANTS LIKE to please you.
- INFANTS LIKE when you are patient, even though they have been fussing for a long time.

What Does The Infant Need From You?

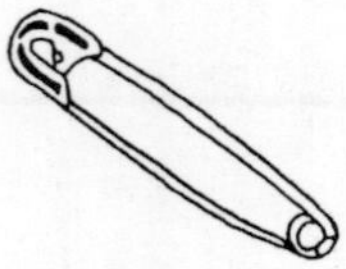

PHYSICAL:

• INFANTS NEED YOU to know how to make them feel physically safe and comfortable. It is important to know how to help the infant feel safe when placed anywhere in your house.

- A safe infant space must provide opportunity for the infant to explore his body, and to use simple toys when awake. Use a variety of equipment designed for infants as ''infant spaces,'' such as a play crib for very young babies (who are not yet crawling) or clean, soft spaces on the floor. Some caregivers use pillows, cushions or a blanket to define their ''infant spaces.'' Walkers, jumpers or infant seats are restrictive, and can be dangerous when left unattended even for a moment.

• INFANTS NEED YOU to know how and when to comfort them when nothing else will work. An irritated or over-excited infant may need gentle holding and talking to in order to calm down.

- INFANTS NEED YOU to respond to their cries for help or attention, as quickly as you can. It is important that infants learn to trust and depend on your assistance when they have a need.
- INFANTS NEED your quick response to their cries. This is the baby's way of learning to communicate, and your response will not ''spoil'' or over-indulge the baby.

• INFANTS NEED YOU to arrange a realistic schedule for their physical care.

- Diaper them several times a day to avoid diaper rash.
- Feed babies when they seem hungry or as requested by parents.
- Secure a quiet area for the infants to sleep.

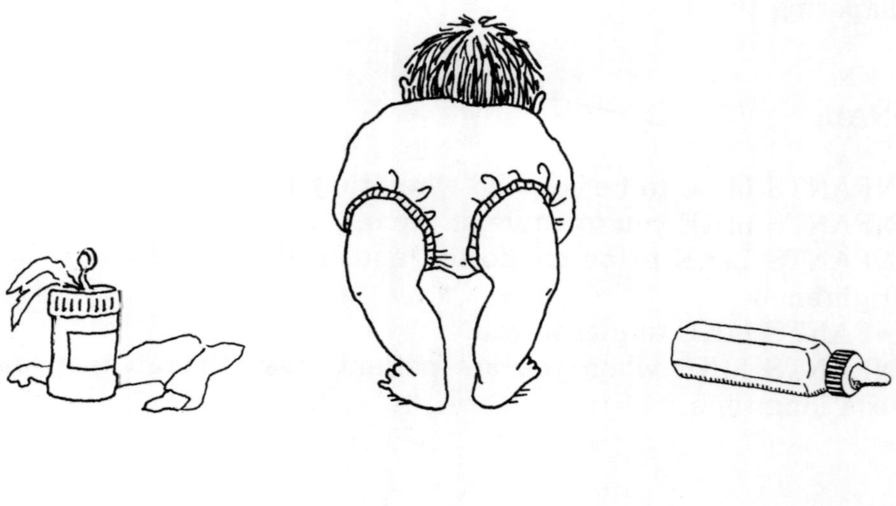

SOCIAL:

• INFANTS NEED YOU to include them in the social climate of your home. The infant wants and needs to be near you and the other children as much as possible during their awake time.

• INFANTS NEED YOU to provide safe spaces where they can observe you and the other children.

• INFANTS NEED YOU to remember that language development starts in infancy. Talk to the infant about what you are doing. For example, *"You look sleepy. I'm going to pick you up and put you to bed for a nap."* Get in the habit of adding words to your actions while you are with the infant. In time, the infant will learn to anticipate and predict what actions and words go together, and what will happen next. Slowly, the infant will begin to understand what the words mean. **By repeating your actions with words over and over again, you are adding to the child's vocabulary and development of language.**

• INFANTS NEED YOU to use other forms of social communication. Singing and the use of simple action songs and games are fun to do with the infant. Simple games like "pat-a-cake," and "peek-a-boo" are old favorites. See Section 4 on Play Activities for more suggestions.

EMOTIONAL:

• INFANTS NEED YOU to know how to soothe, comfort and calm them when they are upset and frightened. Ask parents how they calm their babies. This may or may not work for you. Find ways that will work for you and the infant together.

• INFANTS NEED YOU to communicate your pleasure to them. A smile with a few words can be comforting and encouraging to an infant. A smile with a hug and words is another way.

Remember, the more the infant feels that he is pleasing you, the more he will want to continue to please.

• INFANTS NEED YOU to recognize your own tolerance level with irritable babies. Irritable babies sometimes can fuss and cry for long periods of time. Try to find ways to reduce your own stress.

- If walking and holding the baby does not work, try lying down with the infant. This may calm both you and the baby.

- Try changing the environment. If you are inside, try walking outside. A breath of fresh air may do you both good. (Stay near the door, so the other children can see you.)

- Soothing words can be comforting to the baby as you work through a difficult period. *"I know you don't feel good now, and I am here to help you."*
- Remember that being abrupt or rough with a crying baby will not soothe the crying.
- Your patience and ability to recognize when children need to be alone in order to calm themselves, is one of your many skills.
- When crying babies upset the other children in your home, tell the others that the baby is having a hard day, and you will be able to spend time with them soon.
- Treat yourself to a cup of tea to help with your own stress.

Chapter 4

TODDLER DEVELOPMENT

What Do Toddlers (16 to 24 months) Like?

PHYSICAL:

• TODDLERS LIKE TO practice new motor skills: running, climbing, and of course, falling down.

- Climbing stairs becomes a passion of the young toddler. They will try over and over again to master this challenge. You can provide very low boxes (one foot maximum) and boards for them to step on and off. The gate across the bottom of your stairs can be repositioned to permit young toddlers to go up just one stair, then back down. Toddlers are self motivated, and will need little help "learning" about stairs, if they are allowed to explore and practice with your supervision.

- Falling skills are also being refined and practiced at this age. Toddlers enjoy throwing themselves onto pillows, couches, and each other. They delight in their new abilities to figure out the safety of a situation, and often need your help getting out of situations which are dangerous or scary. Do help toddlers down, and know that they will master the slide another day.

- Running becomes symbolic of their new found mobility. The 16 to 24 month old is experimenting with the newness of viewing the world on two feet. They embrace this discovery, and need time to explore all that they can do.

- TODDLERS LIKE to practice their ability to make things happen.
  - Dropping and throwing small objects.

- TODDLERS LIKE to explore various areas of your home.
  - Opening and closing doors.
  - Filling and dumping objects in containers.
  - Carrying things in purses, lunch boxes, and baskets.
  - Pushing and pulling toys.

• TODDLERS LIKE **Noncommercial Toys:** a cardboard carton, a shoe box, a laundry basket and pillows are all ideal beginnings for creating an appropriate environment for toddlers.

• WATER PLAY AND SAND PLAY continue to be popular. Toddlers learn through their sense. If they can feel it, see it, and hear it, they will want to play and explore. Inside, water play can include taking a bath, washing hands (for a very long time), and ''helping'' with the dishes. Remember, a little bit of sudsy water in a sturdy dish pan is an ideal way to soothe an active toddler.

SOCIAL:

- THE TODDLER will spend long periods of time checking on your whereabouts. They need to re-establish contact, to socialize, and to ask for assistance.

- THE TODDLER copies everything they see the adult do. Toddlers like to imitate and learn from each other. But they will have difficulty sharing toys.

- TODDLERS LIKE to exercise their use of new words. They begin to practice real conversations with family members and their caregivers.

- A COMMON PRACTICE of toddlers is to spend time looking out the window. They are less interested in spending time in restricted areas, and are more curious about what is happening outside. They will spend a lot of time watching people.

EMOTIONAL:

- THE TODDLER LIKES to express affection as well as annoyance to adults.
- THE TODDLER is becoming more interested in peers. This interest will be expressed in pleasure and excitement, as well as feelings of anger and annoyance.

- TODDLERS can display thoughtfulness. They can be very helpful and cooperative at times and will give you a serious nod before toddling off to get that special blanket. These thoughtful behaviors indicate **the beginning ability to understand explanations.**

- THE TODDLER WILL behave in more independent and sometimes "oppositional behaviors." This is part of their natural development to learn more things and to look after themselves. By the time the toddler attains 22 to 24 months, the pressure of "oppositional behavior" lessens.

What Do Toddlers Need From You?

PHYSICAL:

• TODDLERS NEED YOU to develop spaces for "active" movement. The toddler will need large areas to actively explore the physical objects in your home. Provide places for climbing, jumping, and for running. Provide a variety of soft balls for throwing.

• REMEMBER, the simplest toys are often those most enjoyed. Try using old pots, pans, cardboard containers, and lids for stacking. Objects like spoons and corks can be used to fill empty containers.

• LOOK for areas in your home, inside and outside, that can offer opportunities for the toddler to play in water and sand.

• ASSIST THE TODDLER with the beginnings of toilet training. They can be introduced to the "potty chair," and like to sit there fully clothed as they imitate and learn.

SOCIAL

• TODDLERS WILL WANT and need to spend a large portion of each day following you wherever you go. Toddlers will need you to help them master new tasks, to set limits on their active exploration, and be available for simple conversations.

• THE TODDLER WILL WANT to imitate much of what you do. Remember, the toddler is becoming a person, and needs your help to feel a part of the social interactions of your family day care home.

• RESPOND to the toddler's own form of beginning language, i.e. pointing, gesturing, vocalizing and one or two word sentences.

• SHARING TOYS, and sharing you, with other children is difficult for the toddler. The toddler does not have the language, or social skills to engage in social sharing and play. Do not expect the toddler to share toys with other children until his language and social maturity have developed (2½ to 5 years).

- You can help the toddler by letting him or her know which things are possessions, i.e. "her blanket", and don't need to be shared. Also let them know which things belong to your home and will be used by other children.

EMOTIONAL:

• ACCEPT THE TODDLERS' mood swings, between pleasure in mastering new skills and pleasing you, to annoyance and anger when their activities are limited by you. These changes in behavior are normal at this age.

• REMEMBER that toddlers need to be limited and to be protected. They have outbursts of temper, which tend to be short-lived, because their emotions are still immature.

• UNDERSTAND THAT TODDLERS need to try out and do many things, and that they will attempt to do things that they have not mastered.

• TODDLERS have not reached the age where they can wait. "NOW" is the only dimension in time important to a toddler. Realize that toddlers can not wait for many of their immediate needs, and cries of protest are frequent.

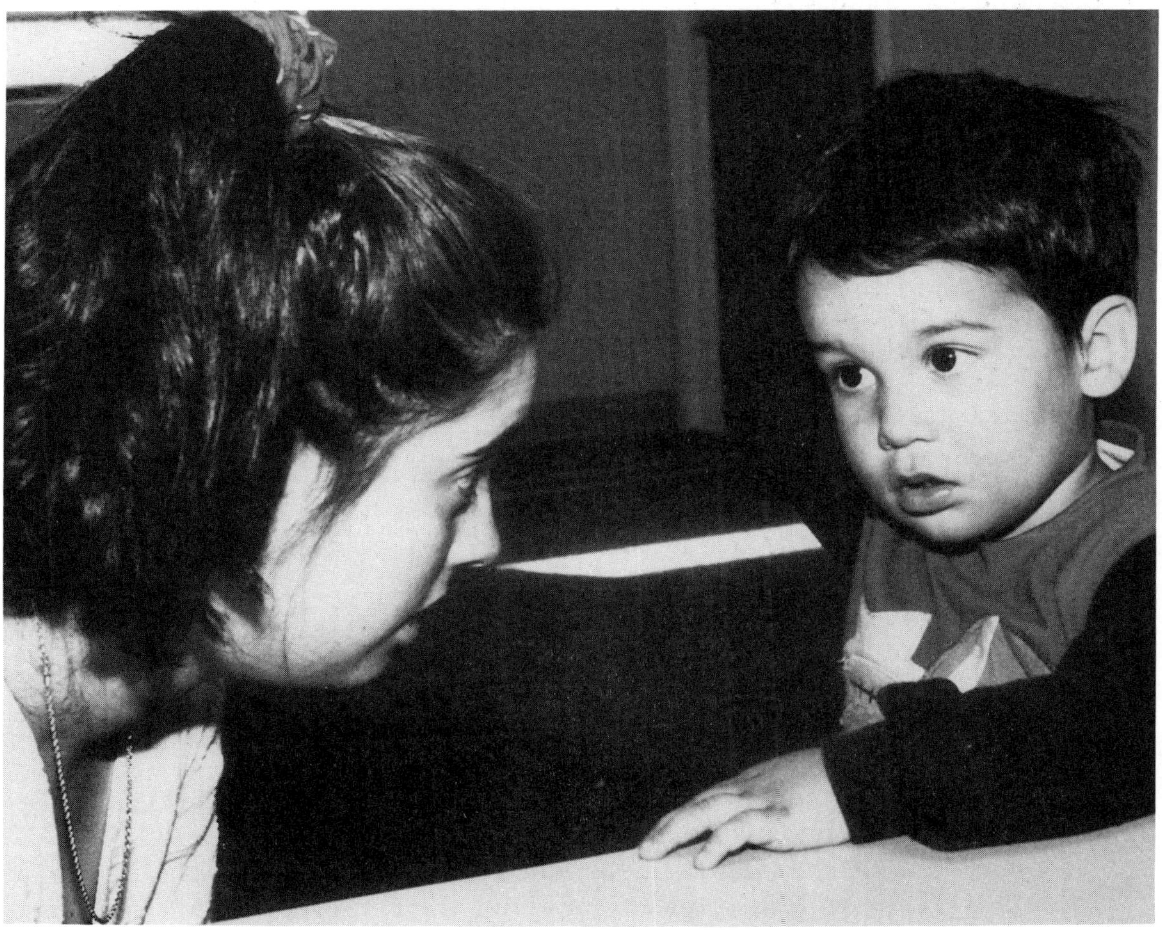

Chapter 5

PRESCHOOL DEVELOPMENT

What Do Preschoolers (2½ to 5 years) Like?

PHYSICAL:

• 2½ YEAR OLDS LIKE to practice and improve upon their new motor abilities. They are better organized than the toddler, and can run and climb with ease. They are more confident and sure of keeping their balance, and are less likely to fall.

• THE PRESCHOOL CHILD continues to improve in motor abilities. By age 3, a child can stand on one foot, dance and jump. And by 4 years, a child can often skip on alternate feet.

• PRESCHOOLERS ENJOY using their newly acquired motor skills. They especially like to:

- Learn by doing. They develop best through motor activities like climbing and exploring.
- Play outdoors. They like an environment which provides for water play, sand box play, digging, and a flat space for wheel toys.
- Develop an understanding of themselves in space. They learn about the limits of their bodies by jumping, running, climbing, turning, swinging, hanging, etc.

• THE PRESCHOOL CHILD LIKES to play with toys and materials that encourage skill and control of eye and hand coordination. The preschool child has more control of fine motor skills and can build a tower of 10 cubes. Their perceptual motor skills improve at this time:

- a child of 2½ can copy a circle
- a child of 3 can copy a cross
- a child of 5 can copy a square

• PRESCHOOLERS are developing a sense of body and feelings about their bodies. This can be observed in these ways:

- They can become quite upset at a small cut or wound. At this age the preschooler often has a keen interest in band-aids.
- They will have vague ideas about the body, and how it works internally. They will have questions about their internal organs and how they work.
- PRESCHOOLERS, by age 3, like to take themselves to the toilet, feed themselves and begin to dress themselves.

SOCIAL:

• PRESCHOOLERS often choose to be with people. They now like making friends, one at a time. Although they may want others to play with them, preschoolers are still self-centered and the play is rarely shared at this time.

• THE 3 YEAR OLD likes to play alongside other children; however, the activities of each child continue to be more isolated. They like playing near other children, but often don't choose to play with others.

• PRESCHOOLERS LIKE fantasy play or role playing, and dressing-up with props to act like parents, grocery shoppers, a doctor or superheroes. Much of the play at this stage is an attempt to copy adults. It is the child's first efforts to practice the skills s/he will need as an adult.

• PRESCHOOLERS, will progress from isolated, solitary play to parallel activity and eventually to "cooperative play."

By age 4 to 5 years, play occurs when there is common activity, with sharing and taking turns, resulting in cooperative play towards a common goal.

- Expect to see preschoolers form strong relationships with a few friends, and exclude others in a group.
- Children of this age like to play with imaginary animals or people.

• PRESCHOOLERS LIKE TO talk, and by age 3, they can talk in sentences. A 3 year old likes to tell a simple story.

- At 2 years the child likes to ask "WHAT?"
- At 3 years the child likes to ask "WHERE?" & "WHO?"
- At 4 years the child likes to ask "WHY?"

• A FOUR YEAR OLD PRESCHOOLER enjoys serious discussions, and asking questions about subjects like birth and death.

• THE OLDER PRESCHOOLER'S language will often contain bathroom and elimination words. With adults, the 4 and 5 year old may try to use swear words to shock and defy authority. Even with friends, you will hear much boasting. *"I'm bigger (better, smarter, stronger) than you are."*

• PRESCHOOLERS ENJOY new experiences. Most preschool children enjoy:

- a well read story, so keep books available.
- songs, rhythms, finger plays (see chapter 4 for ideas).
- learning about the size, shape, color, number and names of objects and things in the environment.
- puzzles which help to give skills in form, color, and size discrimination.

- art activities like painting, gluing, collage and clay, which provide visual and sensory experiences.
- A "housekeeping" corner with dolls, dishes, table, chairs, dress-up clothes for unlimited learning new roles and social growth.

- Building blocks which present problem solving situations to experiment with size, form, balance and creativity.
- Short field trips in the neighborhood, to the grocery store, playground, or just a short walk to the end of the block.

EMOTIONAL:

- 2½ YEAR OLDS can experience strong emotions. They want exactly what they want, when they want it. Waiting is difficult, and everything has to be done in a certain way.
- 2½ year olds can be very demanding and they like to feel they can make decisions. It is not uncommon to hear, *"Me do it myself."* At this stage, children like to do the opposite of what you want.

- The 2½ to 3 year old child can feel insecure, and fear that other children are rivals for their favorite toys, or for your attention and affection. The 2½ year old will spend a lot of time protecting toys, and demanding equal time from you.
- 3 year olds are beginning to feel more secure within themselves. They begin to like to share—both objects and you.

- Preschoolers, age 3 and 4, will want to be like you, as soon as they can learn to trust you. They will want to follow you, and do things to please you.
- Preschoolers like to hear words from you when their behavior pleases you. They **like to be validated** for their growth and more mature behaviors.

- 3½ and 4 year old children can show signs of anxiety when forming new friendships. Children at this age often want to form a strong friendship with "my friend," to the exclusion of other children. They may emphasize a liking for certain children by excluding and refusing to play with certain others. There can be more aggression in play at this age. Children may threaten others or hurt themselves. These aggressive behaviors and feelings can be disturbing to the child.

- Preschoolers may display other signs of anxiety, and release tensions by:
  - nail biting
  - nervous symptoms such as nose picking, sniffling, and coughing.

- Preschoolers will talk of their **fears** of the dark, animals, injury, doctors and death.

What Do Preschoolers Need From You?

PHYSICAL:

• PROVIDE SPACE INDOORS for some active play and movement for the preschoolers. Decide where they can be safe while using their large muscles. A small area in a room, away from furniture, can be used for music games, rhythms and dancing.

• Preschoolers prefer to play outdoors. Provide space outdoors for more active play. Schedule days when you allow for water and sand play. If possible set up areas for climbing and jumping, and for swinging and sliding. If your home or apartment is limited in outdoor space, use a nearby public playground at least twice a week. Remember, preschoolers develop best through **doing** activities.

• Purchase a few wheel toys for the toddler size child and preschooler if space and money permits (or ask parents in your program to donate one). Wheel toys are popular, but are not necessary if your outdoor area does not have a flat surface.

• Select a few, but sturdy, table games that encourage eye-hand coordination.
- Use small building blocks and cubes, interlocking type construction toys, stacking and sorting blocks.
- Use simple puzzles, paper, large crayons, pencils, felt tip pens, etc.

SOCIAL:

• SET UP your indoor space so the children can learn through playing by themselves and with others.

- Use tables for games and activities, like puzzles, stacking, sorting, and paper and crayon use.
- Set aside floor surface for building blocks and construction type play. Use small wheel cars, trucks, play houses, play people and play animals with the blocks.
- Provide a fantasy play area, or a place with dress-up clothes, dishes, dolls and puppets. Children enjoy acting like parents, doctors, nurses, fire-fighters or super heroes, so have old hats, shoes, jackets and night gowns available.

• **HELP 2½ to 3 year olds during the "NO" stage.** Remember this stage of development is normal as children attempt to become more independent both physically, and toward those people who set the limits. It is as though children are trying on their new independent self through negative behavior. Thus, they often say, *"I don't want to."* and *"NO,"* when you or their parents makes a request or sets a limit. Here is how you can help children during this stage:

- Understand what the child is going through. Saying "NO" is an important developmental step towards becoming more independent.
- Remember the child is not "naughty" or "bad" but rather that the behavior, not the child, is unacceptable at times.

• Try to use different ways to "work around" the child's stubbornness and rigid behaviors. Avoid meeting the stubbornness head-on. Don't ridicule or shame the child.

- Keep your routines with the children simple. Avoid unnecessary demands or different expectations from day to day.
- Continue to set firm limits. Avoid situations where the child takes over.
- It is necessary to be **FIRM AND TOLERANT** with children at this stage in order for them to feel successful in becoming more grown-up and independent.

• UNDERSTAND the development of social play between preschoolers.
- 2½ year old children **prefer** to play alongside each other, but not with each other. They are not ready to share play ideas or toys. This stage of social play is called **solitary, or isolated play.**

- 3 year olds are more interested in what other children are playing and will imitate the play of others close-by. This is called **parallel play**. The 3 year old is still not capable of sharing toys.
- 4 to 5 year olds attempt to play with other children. They can decide on their own play ideas, and share toys and materials. This is called **cooperative play.**

• HELP children of this age to be expressive. The preschool child is not a small adult, and learns best by **direct sensory experiences:**

Your program should provide activities which involve opportunities for:
Touching—clay and playdoh
Tasting—a variety of foods (hot or cold)
Seeing—new things in your neighborhood (walks)
Smelling—flowers in your garden, or the soup in the kitchen.
Hearing—new songs and fingerplays
Feeling—sand and what it can do

• As the children explore with direct sensory experiences, talk to them about what they are doing, feeling and learning.
• Give the preschooler opportunities to make choices. For example, *"Do you want to play here with the playdoh, or build with the blocks on the floor?"*

Or, *"It will soon be time for lunch. While I am cooking, do you want to play with puzzles, or be with me in the kitchen?"*
- Giving children choices is another way of avoiding confrontations leading to a "no" response.

EMOTIONAL:

- HELP THE PRESCHOOL CHILD experience a sense of individuality and self control that can lead to a feeling of success, achievement and pride.

  - Avoid punishing the child during this negativistic or oppositional stage.
  - Be firm, but tolerant of this developmental stage.
  - Understand that the preschool child will have toileting accidents from time to time. **Avoid making the child feel a sense of shame when accidents occur.**

- ACKNOWLEDGE with words of pleasure and recognition when the preschooler "pleases" you with learning and growth. For example:

"I like the way you put your toys away all by yourself."

"I like it when you use your words to ask me to help you put your shoes on, instead of crying. I want to help you when you ask for help."

"I saw you take your plate and cup over to the sink all by yourself. Thank you."

"I know that Myesha made you mad when she kicked your blocks. I am glad you could tell her with your words, 'Stop it. I don't like that!' instead of hitting her. Your words made Myesha stop and listen to you."

• UNDERSTAND what is normal and appropriate aggression at this age. Very young children have strong feelings just like adults.

Don't Worry About Normal Aggression:	Be Concerned About:
- The 2½ to 3 year old child who may act out by hitting, kicking or biting. These aggressive behaviors can be within normal range since children this age do not have verbal command of their tensions and anger.	- The 2½ to 3 year old child who strikes out regularly at you and others.
- The pre-verbal child who sometimes resorts to physical aggression.	- The child who may display panic stricken behaviors.
- The 3 to 5 year old child who gets into ''conflicts'' with peers, from time to time.	- Children who have severe temper tantrums, and not only hurts other, but hurt themselves.
- The 3 to 5 year old child who can enjoy fighting...but in a friendly physical way.	- The 3 to 5 year old child who seems to create aggressive situations.
- Children of this age who can settle their own quarrels. As a last resort, remove them from the group. This is effective because the child wants to be with others.	- The child who provokes problems.
	- The child who is ''angry'' or gets upset easily, and is difficult to calm down.

Whenever you feel that a child is displaying behavior that is too disruptive, you should contact your community child care Resource and Referral Agency.

Chapter 6

SCHOOL-AGE DEVELOPMENT

What Do School-Age Children (5 to 7 years) Like?

PHYSICAL:

- 5 to 7 year olds are still very active in their small and large muscle play.
- While 5 year olds are content to stay within the bounds of their physical activity, 6 year olds like new adventures and will try more reckless things.
- 6 year olds tend to be more aggressive with their bodies, and will meet new situations head on.
- 7 year olds seem to slow down their large muscle activity, and are more content to be busy with their hands.
- 7 year olds like to keep busy with pencils, paper and to refine their newly developed fine motor skills.
- Right or left handedness is usually consolidated by age 5.

SOCIAL:

- 5 year olds still like to stay near home. They like to be near the adults.
- 6 year olds begin to move away from family members and begin to seek friends outside their home.
- 6 year olds turn their interest to other adults, such as teachers, scout leaders and others.
- 6 year olds begin to share their interests and ideas more with friends than with family.
- 6 and 7 year olds need and want peers with whom they can play and identify.

- 6 and 7 year olds gradually spend more time with friends than with family.

- 6 and 7 year olds are beginning to be aware that there is a time for play and a time for work.
- 6 and 7 year olds are beginning to prepare themselves for adult roles.

- 6 and 7 year olds feel the impact of school and the bigger community.
- 6 and 7 year olds enjoy team games and board games.

- The play of children between 5 and 7 years is predominatly cooperative:
  - However, expect these children to be rigid and negative with their peers at times, and be able to explode into tears when losing a game.

INTELLECTUAL:

- 5, 6, and 7 year olds are entering into the stage of "concrete operations." This means that they:
  - Can take into account two or more variables, and
  - can differentiate height and weight.

- 5, 6 and 7 year olds take pleasure in discovery and accomplishment. They like to make things for you to demonstrate how much they know.

EMOTIONAL:

- 5 year olds like to do things for adults, and they like to obey adult commands.

- 5 year olds are content to stay within reachable limits, and usually do not want to test the unknown.

- 6 year olds can become very demanding. They can express strong emotions of love and hate to the adult, particularly the mother.

- 6 year olds like to have things done their way.

- 6 year olds can have a difficult time accepting criticism and punishment.

- Mother is no longer the center of the world to the 6 year old.

- 7 year olds might want to be alone more often—to watch television or to read.

- 7 year olds often demand too much of themselves, and can become easily exhausted.

- 7 year olds tend to complain that others don't like them, and that others are picking on them. They can generally express dissatisfaction with life.

What Do School-Age Children (5 to 7 years) Need From You?

PHYSICAL:

• Accommodate the 5 and 6 year old's need for physical activity. Provide time after school for outdoor play, either in your backyard or trips to a nearby park or playground.

• Remember that 5 and 6 year olds need to be supervised out doors, and safety limits and rules need to be enforced.

• Understand the 6 to 7 year olds **readiness** for trying out new and more challenging things. Acknowledge their need to expand physical skills, and reinforce your safety rules.

• Make available an area of your home where school-age children can have a place to play with each other, away from the younger children.
- A large table with chairs (perhaps the kitchen table) is an ideal place for small motor activities like table games, art activities and homework.

SOCIAL:

• 5 year olds want to be near you and assist with tasks, when appropriate. They like to be instructed, and to get permission.

• 6 year olds want to be the center of their world. The adult is now second best. Recognize this behavior as normal and respect it as attempts at personality development.

• Provide areas and materials for school-age children to play together in order to gain skills in socialization.
- Don't place unreasonable limits or restrictions on social group play.
- Have rules and limits for play and activities.
- Allow children to have sufficient contact with other children their age.

• Make snack time a social activity.
- Eating and conversation is a pleasure at this age.

INTELLECTUAL:

- Provide more challenging table games:

checkers	chess	battleship
playing cards	monopoly	chutes and ladders

- Provide quiet spaces for:

homework	reading	sharing of ideas.

- Allow school-age children to unwind after school and engage in play and social games prior to completion of homework assignments.

EMOTIONAL:

- 5, 6 and 7 year olds can be very emotional and explosive at times.
  - Use praise and recognize the explosive feelings of this age group. Group pressures are mounting.

- Avoid using criticism, blame and punishment whenever possible.

Set Reasonable Rules and Limits and Make Them Stick!

- Expect mood swings. If things go well, the child can be a happy and eager player, but if things go badly, there can be tears and tantrums.

- Recognize that ''striking out'' verbally and arrogant behaviors are momentary. They are try outs at becoming bigger. Protect the child from taking on too much and from self-criticism.
  - Don't allow the children to criticize each other.
  - When you show tolerance, they will be able to be more tolerant of each other.

What Do School-Age Children (8 to 10 years) Like?

PHYSICAL:

- 8, 9 and 10 year olds like to challenge their mastery of motor skills.
  - They can stand and balance with ease.
  - They have the coordination to ride a bicycle.

- 8, 9 and 10 year olds take a pride in their physical body and like to take care of it.

SOCIAL:

- 8, 9 and 10 year olds are becoming more disillusioned with their parents. They are more aware of the parents' and other adults' shortcomings.

  - They rely more on companions for support and cooperation.

  - They tend to gang up against the adults and adult authority.

  - Opinions of friends are more important than the opinions of their families.

  - They are more interested in peers for satisfying relationships and their relationships with peers intensifies.

- Team play is very popular. They like to choose teams and decide the rules. Team play can be very absorbing and challenging, (baseball, kickball, soccer, etc.).

INTELLECTUAL:

- School-age children like to initiate new activities.

- They are capable of abstract thought, and can **think** about things.

  - There is a greater capacity for thinking and memory; language skills are better developed.

EMOTIONAL:

- There is a gradual withdrawal from parents and other adults, and an increase of relationships with peers.
  - School-age children begin to keep their secrets for friends and no longer share them with parents.
  - They find pleasure in thwarting the adult as much as possible.

- They can cope better with mature concepts, such as death, birth and sexual and racial differences.

- By 9 and 10 years of age, children can demonstrate a considerable amount of self-reliance and capability.
  - They can delay the expression of an "impulse," and are able to exhibit more control at this age.

- They tend to worry and be anxious about the demands of peers, school and the social community.

What Do School-Age Children (8 to 10 years) Need From You?

PHYSICAL:

- Provide additional physical outlets for the school-age child.
  - Trips to neighborhood parks and playgrounds offer more challenging equipment and apparatus.

  - City recreation programs may provide structured activities at no fee or nominal cost.

  - Check swimming pool programs, libraries and lessons available during summer months which are close to your home.

  - Check your local Y.W.C.A. and Y.M.C.A. for year-round programs.

- Anticipate the changes and swings in activity and mood.
  - At times this age child will have high energy, and activity will be boundless.
  - At other times, this age child will want to hang back, and be with peers to talk, play games or watch television.

SOCIAL:

- Children at this age are attempting to develop as a separate individual as well as develop strong ties with their peers.
  - This is a difficult, ongoing growth task, and there must be a mutual coordination between the developing individual and their social environment.

- Understand the social growth tasks of the 8 to 10 year olds.
  - Allow them to spend time together.
  - Don't require them to assist you in caring for the younger age children. Do so only occasionally, or in an emergency.
  - Provide space and materials for this age child to come together with peers for recreation and socialization.
  - Recognize their wants and needs to have their maturity, independence and separateness respected.

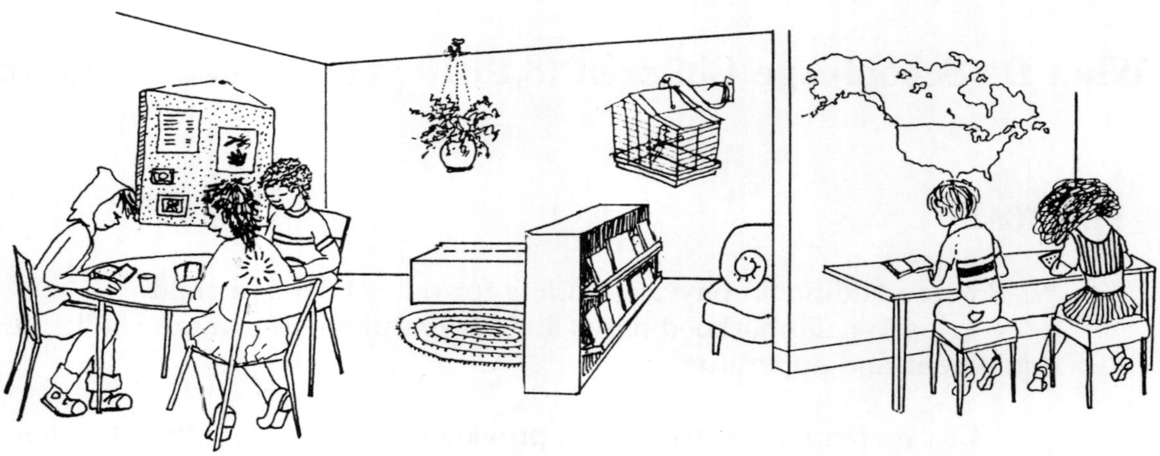

INTELLECTUAL:

- Provide separate space for more quiet activities: reading, table games, talking and sharing of ideas, and completing homework.

- Be available to help with questions they have about school assignments, but do not feel you need to teach them new concepts.

EMOTIONAL:

- Understand the need of this age child to pull away from the adult.

- Reinforce the need for peer contact and relationship.

- Realize that this age child can be anxious and may in fact tend to take things too seriously.
  - They may complain that conditions at school and at home are "too hard."

- Be understanding of this behavior. These complaints may be areas of difficulty for the child, so apply limits accordingly.

Remember that the information provided about child development is also applicable to your own children. Their feelings about other children coming to spend the day in their home will need to be considered. Be sure to introduce them to all new children and give them your assurances that new children will soon calm down and feel comfortable in your home.

The next section will provide some practical applications of child development theory. The day to day issues of separation and feeding are intended to be examples of ways that caregivers rely on their knowledge of the needs and likes of children at different ages.

REFERENCES

Brazelton, B. M.D. *On Becoming a Family*. New York: Delacorte Press, 1981.

——————. *Infants and Mothers*. New York: Delacorte Press, 1969.

Erikson, E. *Child and Society*. New York: W.W. Norton, 1963.

Fraiberg, S. *Clinical Studies in Infant Mental Health*. New York: Basic Books, 1980.

Gerber, M. "Respecting Infants: The Loczy Model of Infant Care" in Jones, E., ed., *Supporting the Growth of Infants, Toddlers and Parents*. Pasadena, CA: Pacific Oaks College, 1979.

Gerber, M. *Resources For Infant Educarers*. Los Angeles, CA: 1550 Murray Circle, 90026, 1979.

Honig, A. and Lally, J. *Infant Caregiving*. Syracuse, New York: Syracuse University Press, 1981.

Rubin, R. *Your Toddler, Ages One to Two*. London: Collier Macmillan, 1980.

NOTES

Section III
PRACTICAL APPLICATIONS OF CHILD DEVELOPMENT CONCEPTS

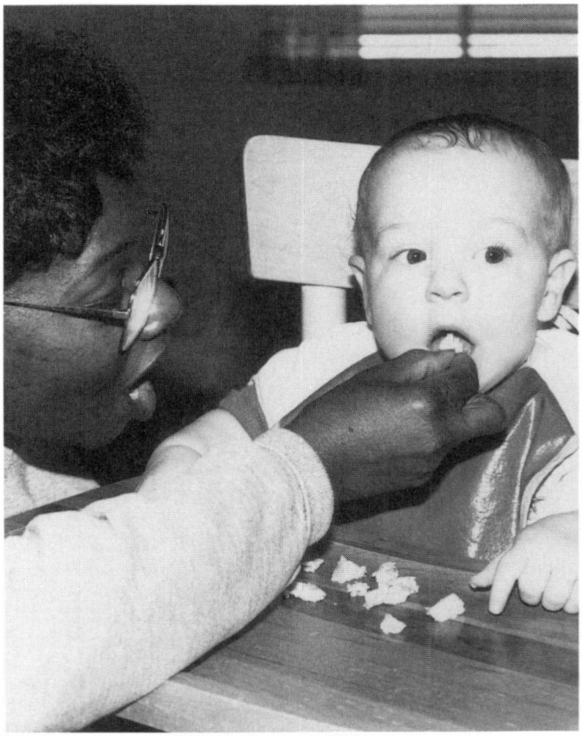

This section describes practical examples of separation and feeding in order to assist you in applying what you know about child development. The way you structure daily caregiving routines is influenced by what you know about what young children need and like.

The way children react to coming into your care depends on many factors including their development and their relationship with their parents. But most importantly it will depend on what you can do to make the adjustment into your home as smooth as possible. Knowing what to expect as they enter your care will enable you to help them feel more comfortable.

Caregiving routines work best when you are aware of the range of developmental needs of each child. This section offers guidelines to caregiving activities like feeding, diapering and putting children down for naps.

The adult task, that of feeding young children, is intended to be an example of ways to provide for the care of children without totally disrupting their self-directed play activities.

Chapter 7

WHEN A NEW CHILD COMES INTO YOUR CARE

The ability and stamina to care for groups of boys and girls for long hours every day is a talent few people possess. People who are sensitive to the needs of children realize what a tremendous responsibility caring for young children can be. Depending on the age of the child, most will react differently to being left at your home by their parents. Their often uneasy reaction is appropriate, and usually gives you information about how the child is struggling with the issues of separation.

Infants (0 to 15 months)

During the first year the infant should be establishing a primary relationship with its parents. Infants depend on their parents for their basic needs—to be fed, to be held, to be soothed and comforted, to be wanted. During these early months of attaching, babies have learned to depend on their mother and father for food, love and warmth.

How children have been cared for during the first months of attachment will affect their behavior when they come to stay in your home. The following guidelines will help you identify what to expect and what to do to ease the transition from one home to another.

WHAT TO EXPECT:

- A well cared for infant will show initial distress when left with a new caregiver. However, the very young infant, under five months of age, will show less disturbance, and sometimes readily accept a new caregiver.

The infant between 7 and 12 months of age will show more stress and perhaps trauma when separated from the parents. This change in behavior is explained as the infant enters into a stage called the **stranger anxiety** period. By seven months of age, the infant has developed an emotional attachment, an awareness of familiar people and things, and the ability to know the difference between the usual caregivers and strangers. They can show their dislike at being placed with strangers. Often this age child will react to the separation with fear, which can result in intense crying and discomfort.

Between 12 and 14 months, the infant begins to separate more easily from the parent. The infant's need to practice newly developed physical abilities, and to explore their environment becomes a motivating force for this separation.

- Realize that these separation feelings and behaviors are experienced by all children.
- Children will naturally be frightened, upset and will take a while to calm down when separated from the parent.
- Understand that most parents will be in stress and upset during the initial separation process. It will take time for them to trust you as the new caregiver. Once they feel more comfortable, you will observe an ease in separation take place for the parent.

Understanding what to expect can help caregivers sympathetically work with families unfamiliar with childcare. The following section discusses a practical approach to caring for new children. These suggestions are based on a two year study by J. Ronald Lally, Ed.D., Director of the Center For Child and Family Studies in San Francisco. Dr. Lally's two year study, ''Minimizing The Trauma of Separation When Leaving A Young Child With A New Caregiver,'' researched the development of trust and persistence in children 0-three years of age. An article by Dr. Lally based on this research appears in the magazine *WORKING MOTHER,* ''Feeling Good About Saying Goodbye,'' August 1985.

Some of the points Dr. Lally made can help you to understand how to respond when a new infant comes into your care.

WHAT TO DO:

1. **TIME:** As a caregiver, you need to give new children TIME to warm up to you and your home environment. The child will need time to judge whether you and your home can be trusted.

   Upon first contact:

   - Resist approaching the infant and making physical contact. It will be easier on the child not to be touched or held by you at the first meeting.
   - Avoid trying to ''make friends'' too quickly.
   - Don't expect the child to talk first, or be able to listen to you.

2. **DISTANCE:** The child will need emotional and physical space to warm up to you at first contact.

   - Allow and insist that the child stay physically close to the parent, when first meeting the child.
   - Avoid close proximity to the parents and the child. The child will feel more at ease if you keep at a distance.
   - The further away the caregiver is at first contact, the better the child likes it.

- Do not stand right next to the child.
- Keep a distance from the parent and child. Use a chair or table as objects to keep a distance.
- Have a conversation with the parent, not the child.
- Avoid asking the child his or her name.

3. **DEGREE OF FAMILIARITY:** The study found that children are affected by the way caregivers look and act. Children will notice differences in appearance between you and their parents. The greater the similarities in appearance between the caregiver and the child's parents, the greater the chance it will take less time for the child to warm up to you.

The child will exhibit more ease or more discomfort depending on the number of pleasant contacts the child has already experienced with new caregivers. If the child's experiences with other caregivers has been positive, the easier it will be for the child to feel comfortable with you.

4. **INTENSITY OF FOCUS:** It is less frightening for the child if the new caregiver establishes first contact in an indirect manner. An indirect focus on the child by the caregiver will lead to a quicker and less tearful separation.

- Focus your attention and conversation directly to the parent, not the child. Avoid asking questions of the child.
- Try not to approach the child too quickly. Allow the child time to naturally come closer to you.
- The child between 12 and 14 months, however, can be more easily attracted to an interesting toy than the younger infant. It is at this stage that the caregiver can use the child's intensity of concentration on one thing at a time to aid in the separation process.

"I think I will put this little car right here on the floor, in case you want to play with it."

Toddlers (15 to 24 months)

The issue of separation and independence continues into toddlerhood. As toddlers, children intensely miss their parents. They still have strong feelings of dependence, but they also need to grow and become more independent on their own. At this age, the very young child experiences a dilemma in wanting to be more independent, yet is still very dependent and in need of the people they trust.

The next section outlines what you can expect when a new toddler comes into your care.

WHAT TO EXPECT:

- The two year old will experience difficulty in separating from the parent. Expect their feelings of loss and missing their parents to be stronger and more intense than the infants.

- The two year old is not easily distracted, and will remember and anticipate separation. The intensity of the protest may upset both the parent as well as the child.

- Expect this age child to need you to spend some time at the beginning of each morning talking about what to expect from the day, and when mommy or daddy will return.

- The toddler will probably experience feelings of loss and separation which may result in outbursts of crying and tantrums occasionally during the day.

- The toddler will want to use you as a secure base from which to explore and then come back.

- Expect a period of adjustment at the beginning of the day for the toddler to be able to explore and settle down to the routine.

WHAT TO DO:

- Be sure toddlers have the opportunity to say good-bye to their parents as they are leaving.

- Help toddlers by telling them that you understand how difficult it is to say good-bye.

- Remind the child that their parents will be returning: *"I know it is hard to say good-bye to your daddy this morning, but he will return after your nap today."*

- Allow the toddler to make the first contact or advance towards you, and away from the parent. The toddler enjoys the power and independence to make choices, either moving towards you or an area in your home that holds an interest for them.

- Be sure your play environment is set up with the appropriate toys and materials to stimulate and hold interest for this age child.

- Be available throughout the day for times when toddlers re-experience the loss of their parents. A gentle word, a warm hug, or an available lap can help soothe those scary feelings.

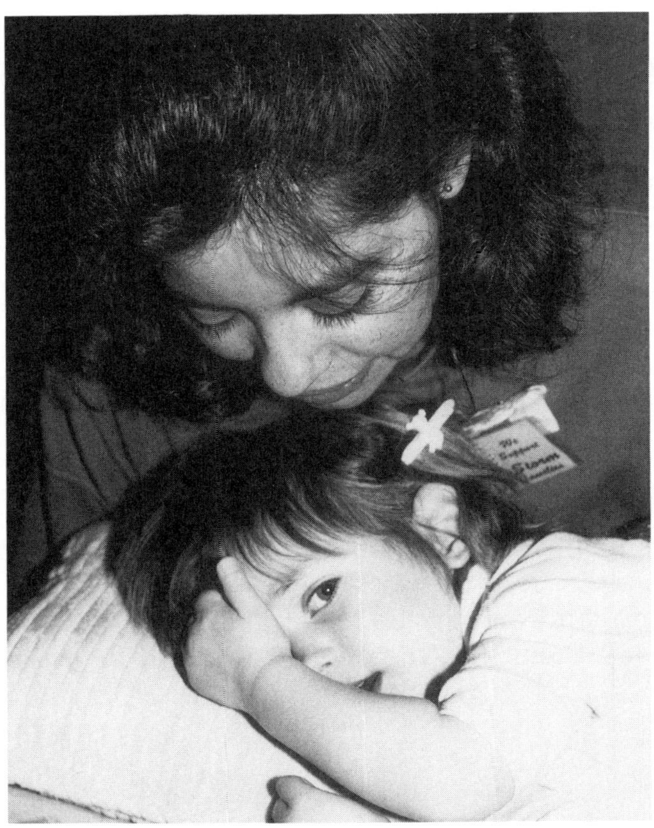

Preschoolers (2½ to 5 years)

The preschool years present some different issues of separation and independence. Toward the end of the second year these differences and their consequences can be clearly seen in the child.

WHAT TO EXPECT:

- The preschooler will attempt to control parents through more clinging and demanding behaviors.

- Children at this age can, however, be more easily reassured about their parents return.

- At the same time, they feel quite free to turn their aggressions onto the exterior world. For example, after the parent leaves, the child may turn around and hit another child.

- Preschool children can be expected to do more things by themselves, like feeding and dressing. Because of their struggle between needing to be dependent and wanting to be independent, you should remain available to help when necessary.

WHAT TO DO:

- Reassure the child that it is hard to say good-bye, and that you understand how scary it is to be in a new place.

    - Make sure they feel welcome to stay close to you while they make this difficult transition.

    - Offer preschoolers one or two choices of things to do, like playing with blocks or looking at a book with you.

- Do not reprimand preschoolers for acting out (misbehaving) because their parents left.

    - Realize that aggresson (hitting, throwing and kicking) may be related to the child's feelings of **loss** through separation from parents.

    - Although children may be upset about not being with their parents, you need to tell them that they cannot hit and express anger by hitting, kicking, etc.

- Offer ways for the child to express in words feelings about loss. *"You can tell me about how mad you are that your daddy has left you."*

• **Tolerate** regressive behavior like wetting and soiling. Although preschoolers can do more and more for themselves, they are still struggling with issues of dependence and independence. *"You just had an accident. I am not mad at you."* Your patience and understanding at this time will help the child trust that you know s/he will have more control as time goes on. *"Let's go change your pants, and I will help you to remember how to go to the bathroom by yourself the next time."*

School Age Children

With the older school-age children in your program, issues of separation shift from separation from parents to attempts to develop as separate individuals and establish relationships with their peers.

WHAT TO EXPECT:

• They will be angry about leaving their peers at school to come to your home.

• They will need to tell you about what happened to them at school.

• They will have high and low moods because of school and peer pressures.

• They will not want to do their homework.

WHAT TO DO:

• Anticipate their arrival by having a snack ready for them.

• Provide a special place for them to eat and visit with you.

• Encourage them to assist you in preparing for their afternoon program of activities.

• Create a place where they can have space to do their homework and be away from the "little kids."

Chapter 8

FEEDING —— A DAILY CAREGIVING ROUTINE

There are times in each day when you must intervene in the play of the children to perform the important tasks of feeding, diapering, toileting, dressing and napping. There are ways to provide for the care and feeding of children in a manner that adds quality to the activity. One approach is to structure the caregiving activities to meet the wide range of individual needs of the various age groupings of children in your care. Consider the basic routine of ''feeding'' to meet the needs of children of different ages.

Guidelines For Caregiving Routines

AGE AND DEVELOPMENTAL NEED OF CHILD

INFANT: 0 to 12 MONTHS

- Infant will show signs of wanting to feed by sucking or fussiness.

- Infant needs a quiet and comfortable place for feeding. Select an area of the playroom that is relatively quiet for the infant, but still allows you to supervise the other children playing.

- Infant learns to anticipate what is going to happen to him by paying attention to your ''words'' and actions.

- Infant responds to you by:
  - looking at you,
  - making sounds,
  - moving body, or
  - all 3 of the above.

WAYS TO STRUCTURE ROUTINES

ADULT TASK: FEEDING INFANTS

- Get to know infant's regular pattern of eating

- Get to know individual ''cues'' for fussiness or sucking, by careful observation.

- Explain to the infant what is going to happen, after you acknowledge his need. *''You seem to be hungry now, David.''*

- Before you leave the room to prepare his food or bottle, tell the infant and the other children (who are engaged in safe play) what you are going to do, *''I am going to the kitchen to get David's bottle. I'll be right back.''* Be sure the other children in your care are all right, and have heard your verbal message.

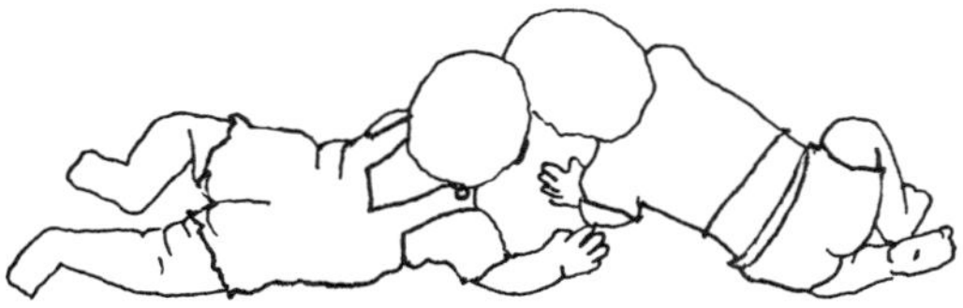

• Infant continues to respond to your words and actions as the bottle comes closer.
- By looking at you
- By making sounds in response
- By making body movements in excitement and anticipation

• Infant will show that he is finished either by pushing the nipple out or turning his head.

• When you are ready to feed the infant, explain what is going to happen. *"I'm going to pick you up."*

• Wait for the infant's response to your words. This approach of treating the infant an an active and capable participant, rather than a passive recipient, provides the infant with intimate contact and quality nurturing from you.

• After the infant responds, pick him up and hold him in your lap to feed him. Show him the bottle, and again explain what is going to happen. *"Look, your bottle is ready and you can eat, David."*

• Wait again for his response to these last words before feeding.

• Be sensitive to the child's pace and temperament.

• Continue to observe infant while he is feeding. He will give you signals when he is slowing down and when finished with the bottle.

• Respect his signals when slowing down, and communicate to him that you think he is finished. *"I think you are finished now and I am going to hold you for a while before I put you down."*

This approach to communication during the caregiving tasks can lead to a sense of cooperation and mutual enjoyment between you and the infant. This approach can be as helpful and satisfying for all the different age groups in your care.

TODDLER: 12 to 29 MONTHS

FEEDING:
Toddlers can be directed to stop their play for eating routines like snack and lunch.

• The toddler is learning to and is interested in feeding himself.

- With these new skills in feeding himself, and new feelings of independence, the toddler may refuse to be fed by the adult.

• Toddlers like the social atmosphere connected with eating and enjoy sitting with peers.

• Toddlers will continue to be active during eating time and attempt to get up and down while eating.
- Toddlers may be able to sit for only brief amounts of time (5-10 minutes).

• Toddlers are beginning to learn the "routine" connected with eating.
- They can wait longer for a snack time or lunch time to arrive.

• Toddlers want to act "big" and learn to master new skills. A toddler:
- Wants to sit at a table with peers.
- Wants to help in preparing snack or lunch.
- Wants to use simple utensils, at times.
- Wants to pour their own drink.
- Wants to clean up after eating.

ADULT TASKS: FEEDING TODDLERS

• Recognize when the toddler is ready to come to the table and sit independently.
- Provide a small sized table and chair which he can climb in and out of by himself.
- Encourage his self-help skills by offering a spoon, or cup or finger foods.

• You will continue to set limits on the toddlers' activity during eating.
- Insist that the toddlers **sit** while eating
- Discourage the toddler from taking food away from the table.

• Continue to explain to toddlers what will happen around the feeding routines.
- Sit at the table with the toddlers and offer help when needed.
- Talk about the food being served.
- Talk about the different varieties and textures of the food.

• Allow the toddler to decide how much to eat and when to leave the table.

• Ask for the toddlers' cooperation in following basic rules:
- Washing hands before and after eating.
- Pouring their own juice (use small pitchers—a large measuring cup is easy to manage).
- Cleaning up after themselves with a sponge.
- Preparing some parts of the snack or lunch.

PRESCHOOLERS: 2½ to 5 yrs.

FEEDING:
Preschoolers can be so absorbed in play at this age and stage of their development that food is not as important as before.

• Preschoolers do enjoy "routines" and like to be included in the preparation of food and the eating rituals.

• Preschoolers can help prepare the food.

• They can assist with setting the table.

• Preschoolers like cleaning up after themselves.

• Preschoolers like to socialize during eating times.
- They are capable of beginning conversations with you and their peers.
- They may dominate and have to be reminded to take turns in talking with each other.

ADULT TASKS: FEEDING PRESCHOOLERS

• Recognize that preschoolers can become so "busy" in their play that they might resist stopping their play to eat.

• Prepare preschoolers for the time when meals will occur. Tell them 5 minutes ahead of time, so they will have a warning to get ready for snack or lunch.

• Preschoolers need little help with feeding themselves, but continue to sit at the table with them and offer help when needed.

• Socialize, and continue to talk about what is happening during eating time.

• Comment on the food's taste and smell. Encourage preschoolers to taste new foods, but allow them to decide how much to eat.

AGE/DEVELOPMENTAL NEEDS OF CHILD:

SCHOOL-AGE: 5-10 YEARS

FEEDING: School-age children look forward to eating.

- Appetites tend to increase between 5 and 6 years.
- They like choices and have an acceptance of a wider variety of foods.
- They can use utensils, including spreading with a knife.

- By 6 years, appetites may be tremendous.
  - They may eat better between meals.
  - The school-age child may have strong preferences for certain foods.

- They may want and ask for larger servings than they can eat.

- By 8 to 10 years, appetites and quantities of food increase again.

- Acceptance of all foods is increasing from 8 years of age on.

WAYS TO STRUCTURE ROUTINES—ADULT TASKS: FEEDING SCHOOL-AGE CHILDREN

- Recognize the need of school-age children to want to be fed a snack or lunch, immediately upon returning from school.

- Encourage self-help skills.

- Organize an area in the kitchen for school-age children to assist themselves in food preparation, and cleanup.

- Set rules as to how they can assist themselves
  - Is the refrigerator accessible to them?
  - Are eating utensils available?
  - Are set up and cleanup rules clear and realistic?

- Recognize the increased need for bigger quantities of food, but know how to set limits.

- Include school-age children in food selection and preparation.

REFERENCES

Ames, L. and Ilg. L., *The Gesell Institute: Child Behavior.* New York: Barnes & Noble, 1972.

Auerbach, S. *The Whole Child: A Sourcebook.* New York: Perigee Books, 1981.

Erickson, E. *Childhood and Society.* New York: W.W. Norton & Co., 1969.

Gerber, M. ''Infants' Expression—The Art of Becoming'', *Psychiatry and Art.* Basel, Switzerland and New York, Vol. 3 (1971): 170-175.

Gonzales-Mena, J., and Eyer-Widmeyer, D. *Infancy and Caregiving.* Palo Alto, CA: Mayfield Publishers, 1980.

Lewis, M. *Clinical Aspects of Child Development.* Philadelphia: Lea & Febiger, 1982.

Oku, C. ''Individualization of Routines in Day Care'', *Educaring.* Resources for Infant Educarers, Los Angeles. Los Angeles, (1981) Vol II, Number 2, Spring.

Pikler, E. and Tardos, A. ''Some Contributions to the Study of Infants' Gross Motor Activities.'' *VI International Congress of Applied Psychology* Amsterdam: Swets and Zeitlinger, 1969.

Segal, M. *Your Child At Play.* New York: New Market Press, 1985.

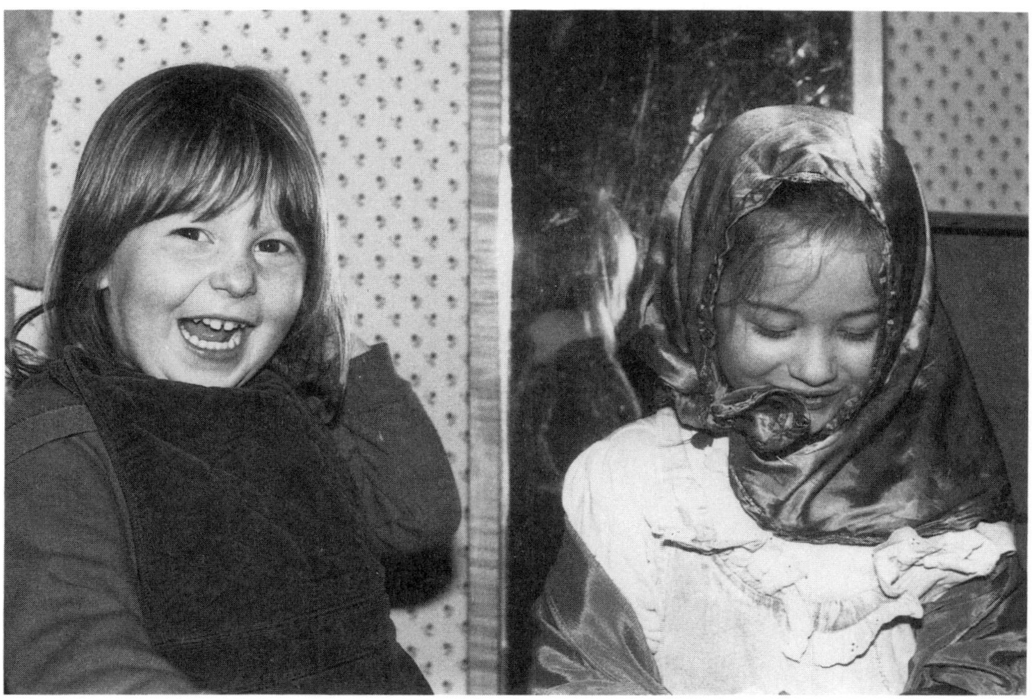

REFERENCES

[illegible] and [illegible]. The [illegible] Service & [illegible], [illegible].

[illegible] The [illegible] New York [illegible].

[illegible] [illegible] 1983.

[illegible] The [illegible] and [illegible].

[illegible] [illegible] and [illegible] [illegible] [illegible].

[illegible], M. [illegible] [illegible].

[illegible] [illegible] [illegible].

[illegible] and [illegible] [illegible].

[illegible] 1986.

Section IV

PLAY-LEARNING ENVIRONMENTS FOR YOUNG CHILDREN

"Play, as we are beginning to understand, is the way the child learns what no one can teach him."

Lawrence K. Frank

Chapter 9

THE VALUE OF PLAY

The study and observation of the value of play began more than 100 years ago when Frederick Froebel started programs of early childhood education in Germany. Froebel called his school for young children kindergarten. The name kindergarten was given to symbolize the care or direction to be taken in helping children grow. Froebel's approach to early childhood education was to observe the play activities of the children in order to determine the program.

In the 1920's, a movement began in the United States to reform kindergarten programs. At this time nursery schools had their beginning, and a new breed of educators developed and applied their ideas about the value of play and learning for children. The educators saw that **what children do while playing is real. It has value, and has within it the potential for learning about oneself and the world.**

Today, early childhood programs have expanded to incorporate what we already know about play and children. Today an observer in most early childhood programs can see how the natural activities of children take place in educational programs. The provisions for dramatic play activities, a housekeeping area, an area for block building, symbolic toys for fantasy play and areas for small and large muscle development all serve as legitimate educational activities for play and learning.

Jean Piaget, and other well known child development theorists, have looked at children's play to explain better how children learn. Piaget demonstrated that much of what we call play is really the activity of intelligence.

> Piaget has defined three distinct stages in the development of play. The first is the sensorimotor stage of infancy, based upon existing patterns of physical behavior. The second is a level of symbolic play, the stage of dramatic play in which we find most nursery/kindergarten children. The third stage is the stage of playing games that have rules, representing the play behavior of older children. As children mature through the early childhood period, they engage in more of this role-playing behavior, developing more of a game orientation along with a lessening of the dramatic play. Play, according to Piaget, is a way of taking the outside world and manipulating it so that it fits the person's organizational scheme. As such, play serves a vital function in a child's developing intellect and continues to some extent in adult intellectual behavior. (Doris Sponseller, *Play As A Learning Medium*).

Lawrence K. Frank, an authority in human development, has also researched the importance of play:

> Play, as we are beginning to understand, is the way the child learns what no one can teach him. It is the way he explores and orients himself to the actual world of space and time, of things, animals, structures, and people. Through play the child practices and rehearses endlessly the complicated and subtle patterns of human living and communication which he must master if he is to become a participating adult in our social life.
> (Ruth E. Hartley and Robert M. Goldenson, Ph.D., *The Complete Book of Children's Play*).

Regardless of the concern for children and the growing recognition of the importance of their play, many people are still not clear about the meaning of play, and what the child needs for his or her playing.

Some important questions which caregivers usually ask are addressed in the following section.

Chapter 10

QUESTIONS AND ANSWERS

Creating play-learning environments in homes is not always easy. If you are a parent of young children, you already know that you must set your own limits in terms of how much you let their toys invade your life.

As a proprietor of a small family day care business in your home, this balancing act becomes more complicated. The needs and wishes of your own family must be considered when you think about rearranging the living room, dining room, etc..

The following section discusses frequently encountered problems about creating environments for play in the home. Consider the questions and answers carefully, so you will be prepared to answer them when others ask you these questions.

WHY DO CHILDREN PLAY?

We know that children have always played. Child development research clearly states that the young of all species play. These facts suggest that play serves some valuable function in the preservation of the species.

Modern theories state additional reasons for children's play. They suggest it functions: (1) as an activity done for its own sake, (2) as more than just the release of energy, (3) as a preparation for future work and (4) as activities. Children use play to cope with the problems of living.

Adults who live and work with children know that children's play is often very serious. Children's play takes on the quality of an intense and absorbing experience. In addition, the meaning of the play experience is unique and special to each child.

Because the essence of the play experience is internal and individual for each child, it may not be obvious or easily understood by the adult who observes the course or form of each child's play activity. Even though adults cannot fully understand it, we can appreciate the seriousness and concentration the child brings to the play experience.

WHEN DO CHILDREN START PLAYING?

Exploration of the environment begins when the newborn enters the world. The turn of the head or the kick of a foot may well be a child's first play.

As you watch the babies you care for, you will notice how much they enjoy lying on their backs and reaching for a colorful scarf. They kick and reach and wiggle all at the same time.

As babies squeeze and touch the objects around them, or as the ball rolls away and under the couch, they begin to realize that objects are permanent and solid. This idea of object permanence is an exciting discovery.

Imitation is another early stage of play. Youngsters enjoy copying you and older children. They want to carry your purse and wear your shoes. They want to draw with the older children, and get into their "stuff."

Your home is their play-learning environment. Just as little ones learn from older children, these same older children have much to learn from the younger ones. *"Gently, play gently,"* you say, as older children touch and play with the babies.

HOW DO CHILDREN LEARN FROM THEIR PLAY?

There are many ways to discuss how play can serve educational functions. One of the best ways to describe how children learn is to outline carefully what we observe children **doing** as we watch them play.

Consider a girl playing in your yard. She wanders from one activity to the other, seemingly without purpose. But as you watch what she is doing, you can begin to formulate some ideas about what she is learning from her play.

WHAT IS THE CHILD DOING AS WE WATCH HER PLAY?

1. She is finding out about physical materials.

- Stacking blocks on top of each other and knocking them down
- Pouring water from one container to another
  * filling and emptying
- Squeezing a sponge
- Running water through a colander
- Using water to wet things
  * sand or earth
- Running sand through her fingers
- Building sand into piles and digging holes
- Trying to lift heavy things
- Throwing light things into the air to see if they float or fall to the ground
- Fitting things together and taking them apart
  * puzzles
  * blocks
  * stacking toys
  * nuts and bolts

2. She is finding out about herself in relation to the world around her.

- In dramatic play, she no longer has to be a child.
- She imitates the adults.
- She plays at being father and mother.
- She can be a wolf, a firefighter or a baby who is crying.
- Dolls and animals become children she feeds, clothes, teaches and punishes.

3. She recreates situations that turn up in her life through play.
- a visit to the doctor or dentist
- an accident, a death or the loss of a pet

WHAT IS SHE LEARNING IN HER PLAY?

1. She is discovering through her manipulation of objects about the nature of materials:
- She is beginning to form concepts of:
  * **weight**—light and heavy
  * **height and size**—tall, short, big, small
  * **texture**—soft, hard, fine and coarse

* She is discovering the possibilities and limitations of her own powers.

- she can hold clay and play-doh, but water runs away

- she can hold wet sand, but dry sand runs through her fingers

- she can break a stick but not a metal spoon

- she is experiencing pleasure and satisfaction in what her hands can make of the physical world

2. By pretending to be father of mother she begins to understand what it is like to be a parent, and can begin to understand their behavior.

3. In reliving and dramatizing the sequence of a painful event, (the fear and trauma of a hospital experience, or the loss of a pet), she can learn to deal with the event. The situation may be reenacted many times until the whole experience is brought into focus and control.

HOW DO I KNOW IF CHILDREN ARE LEARNING FROM THEIR PLAY?

Children learn from experience. They practice and experiment. For instance, you have seen babies drop things from the highchair while the parent retrieves them. The baby, delighting in the experience, will do this over and over again to learn about objects and spacial relationships.

This repetition and experimentation is the way children learn from their play. You will know when the children are learning by the way they approach and solve problems.

One of a young child's most exciting learning experiences is the mastery of walking up and down stairs. Steps are like a magnet for a young child, drawing the youngster to a challenge. Steps demand experimentation and practice, while at the same time provide increased mastery and challenge.

Preschool children will need to repeat the same activity until they have mastered the skill. They will return to the tricycle over and over again...first pushing it with their toes on the ground, then experimenting with their feet on the pedals with jerky movements exploring how to coordinate the steering.

The **process** of mastering the tricycle is an important part of learning. If we try to teach children how to pedal a tricycle, without letting them experiment, we are in essence robbing them of the process of learning.

SHOULD MY ENTIRE PROGRAM DAY BE DEVOTED TO PLAY?

You will recognize the importance of having available a variety of play-learning activities throughout the day. However, the activities necessary to take care of children include more than play.

Your daily tasks include other important caregiving activities like establishing routines for feeding, napping and diapering children. Your challenge will be to balance and integrate the play-learning activities with the caregiving routines in order to have a well-rounded program.

WHAT ARE MY TASKS IN SETTING UP A GOOD PLAY-LEARNING ENVIRONMENT?

The play-learning environment described here explains how you can structure your home to provide children with choices which will enable them to be self-directed in their play activities.

The planning and set up of the play environment.
ADULT TASKS: Structuring the Learning Environment for Free Choice

- Begin by looking at your play environment from a child's point of view.
  - Remember, everything that is present is a potential stimulus for the child.
  - Everything present in the environment, the toys, materials and arrangement of furniture, communicates to the child how to behave in that area.
  - Make available in each room only those play materials that children are free to play with and touch.
  - Put away any personal items or furniture that children cannot touch.

- Define and arrange your physical environment with the children in mind:
  - Arrange the indoor space, i.e. furniture, play equipment and toys, so that children know where they can play.
  - Locate play areas so that noisy and quiet activities can happen without disturbing children. Be sure there is an appropriate place for each.
  - Use area rugs to cut down on noise. A rug under blocks or tables can help. Be sure area rugs are secure and safe.

  - Use low, open shelves so play materials are available when children want to use them.
  - Arrange materials so they are well spaced and uncluttered on shelves.

  - Provide only toys and materials that are in good condition.
  - Provide more than one of the more popular toys to avoid unnecessary waiting and sharing.

- Provide an area for fantasy play.
- Provide an area for art activities. Include cutting, gluing, coloring and painting materials.

- Create an area for language stimulation—a reading area with children's books and stories. A rug and some soft pillows near the books can stimulate conversation between you and the children.

- An area for listening to records, simple finger plays and singing and dancing.

- Plan the outdoor environment, keeping in mind the same guidelines as used in structuring the indoor area.
  - Provide for clear boundaries between very active and semi-moderate activities.
  - Swings and slides should be away from the "traffic areas" used for tricycles and other wheeled toys. They should be safely secured in the ground and at least six feet from fences or walls.
  - Provide for semi-active activities like sand and water play away from more active areas.
  - Plan for safety and ease of supervision of activities.

DO YOUNG CHILDREN NEED TO GO OUTSIDE EVERY DAY?

Yes. It is a good idea for them to be outside as often as possible, weather permitting. They eat more heartily and nap more soundly after playing actively outside. Their spirits and yours will be higher.

A walk to the corner and back can provide some change from the inside play-learning environment. If you have a fenced yard, be sure to take safety precautions (see chapter 1). Some caregivers include outside time in their daily routines, and often serve lunch or snack outside.

WHEN SHOULD ADULTS INTERVENE IN THE PLAY OF CHILDREN?

After the physical environment is set up for play and learning, the adult can step back and supervise the children playing with the materials and each other. Presented here are some guidelines to help adults know **when to** and **when not to** intervene in the play of children.

WHEN TO Intervene in The Play of Children

- Step in to enforce limits and clarify rules.
- Step in to limit the number of children participating in an activity at any one time.
- Step in when a situation is not safe for a child.
- Step in when a child is out of control.
- Be available to offer help with your words and limits when children have conflicts with each other.
- Step in when a child is "stuck" in his play and needs to be redirected.
- Step in when you need to reassure a child about the fairness of taking turns. Set up a system for taking turns.
- Step in when you must involve a child in a caregiving task, i.e., toileting, diapering, etc.
- Step in when you must stop the free play to engage children in an adult directed activity like preparing the children for lunch or snack, napping or taking a walk.

OBSERVATION IS THE KEY

WHEN NOT To Intervene

- Don't step in when you know the children can solve their own problems.
- Wait after the expression of need to allow enough time for the children to solve the problem alone.
- Don't step in when children feel "safe," emotionally and physically with each other.
- Don't step in when children feel and act in control of the physical environment. For example, when children know the rules, and when children know that you are available if you are needed.
- Don't step in when you think the children can learn best from one another.
- Don't step in when the children are motivated and interested in their self-directed play.
- **Don't needlessly interrupt the play of children.**
  - There will be less need to intervene as you reinforce, with your attitude and actions. Respect the children's rights to play alone or with others as you quietly observe.
- Don't over schedule the day with adult oriented activities.
  - There will be fewer times to intervene and discipline if you **allow ample time** each day for children to make and act on their own choices for play and learning.

WHAT ARE APPROPRIATE PLAY-LEARNING ENVIRONMENTS FOR INFANTS?

From the youngest age, infants are exploring and learning. They see, taste, hear and touch; they wiggle, stretch, cry and suck, all in an attempt to figure out the world around them.

They are a bundle of reflexes. Infants learn by organizing information they get from their experiences. For example, infants learn about objects by putting them into their mouths to feel and taste them.

Thus, activities in your home which are best suited for infants are those activities which encourage them to use their senses. Babies are learning so much during the first two years, that all of their experiences become an occasion for learning.

The infant's world is often a wealth of stimulating activities. Your songs and voice as you speak to them during the day provides the beginning lessons of language and communication. The more time you spend talking to them, the more they will learn.

They also enjoy looking at you and watching what is happening around them. Infants prefer looking at faces, and will turn to watch things which slowly move across their field of vision, whether it is other children or a ball rolling across the floor.

As they get older, babies enjoy playing with soft, colorful toys which can be held in their hands. This discovery of their hands enables infants to incorporate holding and touching into their range of learning activities. They will want to taste and touch and look at all the different things in your home.

It is not necessary to buy many special toys for babies at this age, because a wooden spoon and a colorful bandana scarf are wonderful "toys." They taste and feel different, and also make different sounds when dropped on the floor.

All of us have marveled at the rate an infant develops during the first three years of life. Much of this growth is gross motor development. Predictable milestones, such as crawling, sitting, walking and jumping occur during this time. As adults it is tempting to help them reach these milestones. **Yet each time we place them in a posture or position they cannot get into by themselves we are taking away from their sense of mastery and accomplishment.**

Infants are also learning new skills as they twist and stretch to reach for a toy. How tempting it is for adults to just reach out and help. But stop and **think** about all the things a baby learns when reaching for a toy.

First, she is learning that her body moves as a unit. Watch as she reaches with her whole body...from the tips of her fingers to the ends of her toes. Her entire body is involved in reaching for the toy. This stretching helps to tone the body's muscles, especially in the abdomen and back, which she will need later for crawling and sitting.

In addition to feeling the surface under her as she wiggles to reach the toy, she is also getting a sense of her body's capacity to influence her environment. She is learning about the length of her body and how it moves in space.

She is also learning about herself and her abilities to solve problems.

WHAT DO I NEED TO DO TO MAKE CHILDREN FEEL SELF-CONFIDENT IN THEIR PLAY?

When planning learning activities for infants and toddlers, it is important to remember that they enjoy doing things which make them feel self-confident.

An art activity which is too complicated or a song with too many words is a frustrating experience. Activities for very young children are those which make them feel competent and special.

For example:

1) **WASHING TOYS** in a pan filled with one or two inches of warm soapy water allows the child to ''help'' you clean up.

2) **PUTTING TOYS BACK** into the basket after they have been dumped out gives them an opportunity to cooperate and please you.

3) **MUSIC AND SINGING** activities can include pounding and clapping and finger plays. They are often happiest just to hear you clap while singing each syllable of their name.

Remember, infants and toddlers are learning from all of their experiences. They learn through their senses and by moving their bodies. A review of the above three activities indicates the wealth of everyday sensory learning. A basin filled with warm soapy water feels slippery and tastes yucky. Getting toys back into the basket requires special aim and coordination of motor skills. And listening to songs and clapping hands adds a dimension of responsiveness to language development.

HOW DO I JUSTIFY MY USE OF A PLAY-LEARNING ENVIRONMENT FOR CHILDREN WHEN THERE IS PRESSURE AND STRESS ON EARLY ACADEMIC LEARNING?

If you recognize that play contributes to all types of learning, you have accepted a point of view that play is an essential medium for learning. This point of view is a legitimate response to pressures placed on you to introduce early academic learning before young children are ready to engage in formal academic tasks. Since the importance of early experiences have been documented by the majority of educators and psychologists, there is available to you and your parents a wealth of written material about the importance of play in relation to learning. Play is children's work.

In addition, once your own play-learning environment is developed, it may be desirable to invite parents and others to observe children learning while they play in your home.

WHAT TOYS DO I NEED? ARE THEY EXPENSIVE? HOW MUCH MONEY DO I NEED TO SPEND?

If you have already received a license or registration certificate from the state for your family day care home, most of the expense (first aid kit, fire extinguisher, and smoke detector) of setting up an appropriate play-learning environment has already been incurred.

Additional play materials which you add will enhance the quality of your program. There should be a range of age-appropriate toys. Think about the difference between things you buy and things you can make. For example, you need to buy tennis balls and inflatable beach balls, but you can make large pillows for the children to sit on. You need to buy art materials (crayons and felt tip pens), but you can save plastic containers.

Children need toys (not too small around babies) which they can hold and manipulate. A ring of old keys or a set of plastic measuring cups are readily available in most homes. Consider asking for used toys from some of your friends and neighbors, but also know that you will need to purchase new materials throughout the year. Book pages get torn, and puzzle pieces are lost, so it is a good idea to budget about $25 per month to buy toys or to save for a large piece of equipment.

IS IT HARD TO MAKE HOMEMADE TOYS FOR THE CHILDREN?

Making toys is easier than you think. It is surprising that there are so many materials in a home which can be made into attractive, safe and inexpensive toys.

On the following pages, you will find a list of things that you can use for making toys. If you are one of those people who feel lacking in imagination, this is your chance to prove yourself wrong. Dig out some old clothes, get some glue, paper plates, colored beads, yarn, etc., and get the whole group involved in an activity which is both rewarding and fun.

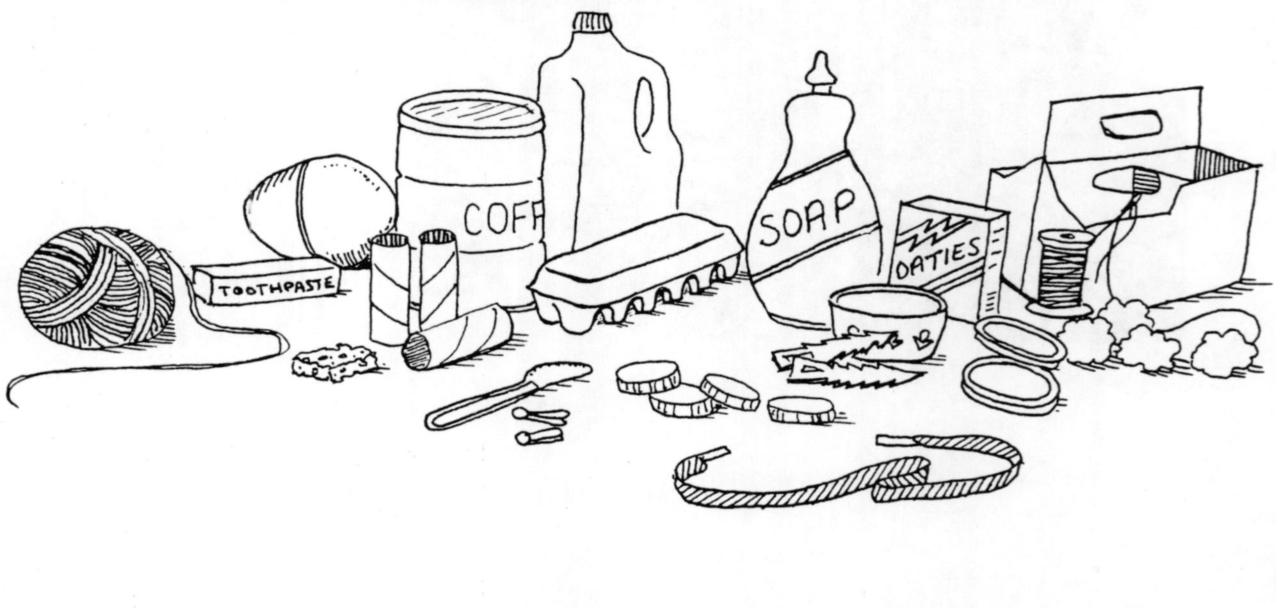

HANDY TO SAVE

SCRAPS OF...
- ribbon
- string
- paper
- yarn
- cardboard

CONTAINERS
- oatmeal, cornmeal and grits cartons
- margarine tubs
- berry baskets
- egg cartons
- cans of all sizes
- cardboard boxes
- cardboard grocery trays
- cardboard tubes from toilet tissue, paper towels and hangers

THINGS FOR PUPPETS
- mittens
- socks
- cloth scraps
- gloves
- nylons

DRESS UP CLOTHES
- old hats
- jewelry
- shawls
- shoes
- ties & belts
- old dresses, skirts

ODDS AND ENDS
- buttons
- spools
- rocks
- cards
- beans
- macaroni
- popsicle sticks
- jar lids
- bottle caps
- keys
- stamps
- straws
- rice
- toothpicks
- corks

DON'T FORGET
- newspapers
- magazines
- paper bags of all sizes
- shirt cardboards

HANDY TO BUY

- Crayons
- Pencils
- Scissors
- Food coloring
- Construction paper
- Crepe paper
- Glue (Children eat paste)
- Masking or transparent tape
- Watercolor or tempera paint (not permanent)
- Felt tip markers

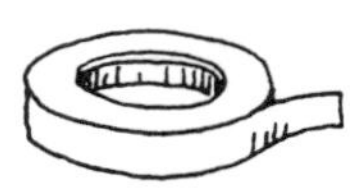

NOTE:

BUY ONLY THE ESSENTIALS!
Try to save as many usable items as you can.
DON'T THROW IT AWAY
—**SAVE IT!**

SHAPE SORTING CAN

With an exacto knife or sharp scissors, cut out (circle, square, triangle) one, two or three shapes from plastic lid of a 2 lb. coffee can.

You may rotate lids or remove the bottom of can and put a simpler lid on one side and a more complex lid on the other.

To make your can more attractive, adhere a piece of contact paper to the outside. Accumulate various shaped household objects to be sorted.

MILK CARTON BLOCKS

Wash thoroughly, then cut off tops of two milk cartons at the same place. Slip one carton into the other, open sides facing. Vary block sizes.

Cover with colorful contact paper or draw a number or shape on each side and cover with clear contact paper.

CLATTER PULL-TOY

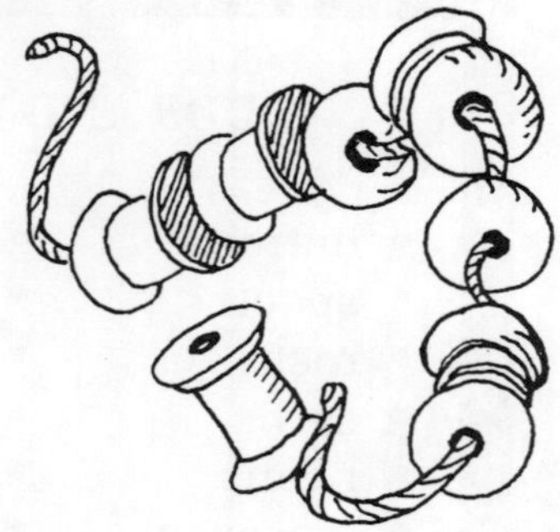

Color spools, mix in some large beads and have the children thread them on a piece of yarn.

SHOE BOX TRAINS

Cover empty shoe boxes, cardboard vegetable trays, milk or egg cartons with comics or construction paper. Draw or cut out windows on some boxes.

Cut out and glue cardboard circles or buttons onto the boxes' sides for wheels, or tape cardboard tubes or spools underneath.

Poke a small hole in the front and back ends of each box; tie a knot at one end of a long string and run it through all the boxes, allowing enough string for pulling.

AGE GROUP: Infant, Toddler

SANDWICH BAG PICTURE BOOK

Using zip-locking plastic bags, create your own books from photographs of the children, their drawings or magazine pages.

"Books" may be wordless or may incorporate words or simple sentences. These books are an excellent opportunity to teach multi-cultural life styles and they may be chewed and drooled on.

MAIL SORTING GAME

Use tissue boxes or shoe boxes covered with pictures and clear contact paper. Cut slot for mail. Choose categories: clothes, food, transportation or colors. Glue various pictures from chosen categories on envelopes to be sorted into "mail boxes." Children may sort them according to categories or by beginning consonant sounds.

CLOTHESPIN WORDS

Print an alphabet letter on each wooden clothespin. Include extra vowels and common consonants. Make words by snapping the clothespins onto a hanger.

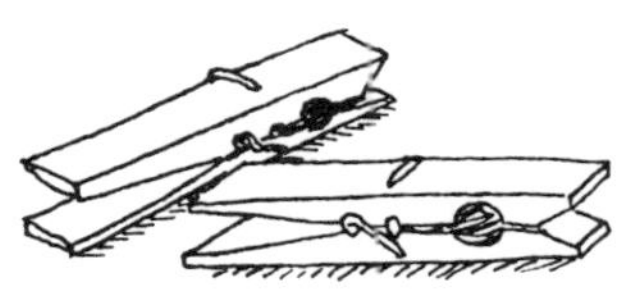

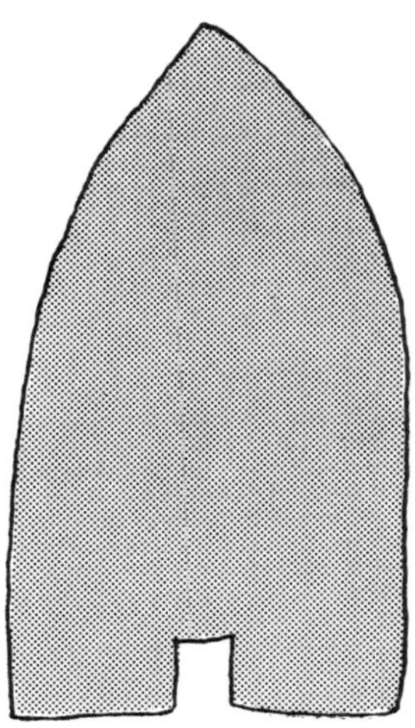

BOAT WITH SOAP POWER

Use this pattern to cut out a boat from a styrofoam meat tray. Save your left-over soap slivers and place one into the slot at the back of the boat.

Fill a shallow pan with water and wait until the water is very still. Drop boat onto the water and watch it go!

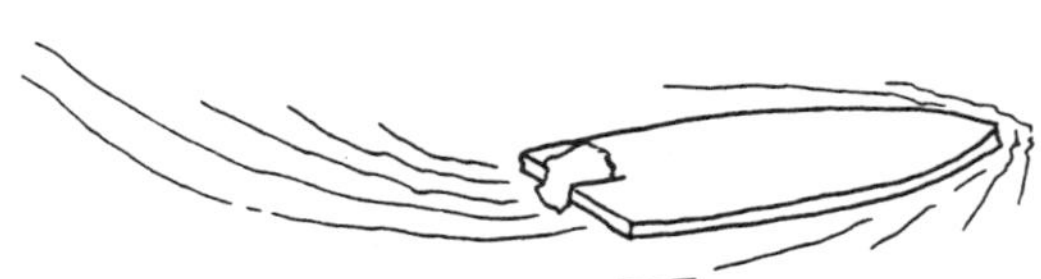

AGE GROUP: Preschool, School-Age

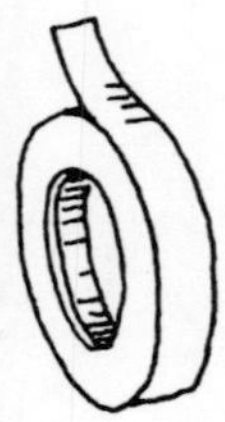

I HAVE HEARD THAT ART ACTIVITIES ARE FUN FOR CHILDREN, BUT WHAT ABOUT THE MESS?

As we know, children learn by experimentation. Every child has an innate desire to explore with her hands and eyes, and to express herself freely through a wide range of materials. As the child grows, she learns to coordinate her body movements, and increase her mastery of large and fine motor skills. Coordination is perfected through basic movement patterns and explains why the eye-hand activities required in most art activities are important to the overall development of children. You will learn to accept some of the mess that comes with providing art opportunities for children as you watch their growth and enjoyment.

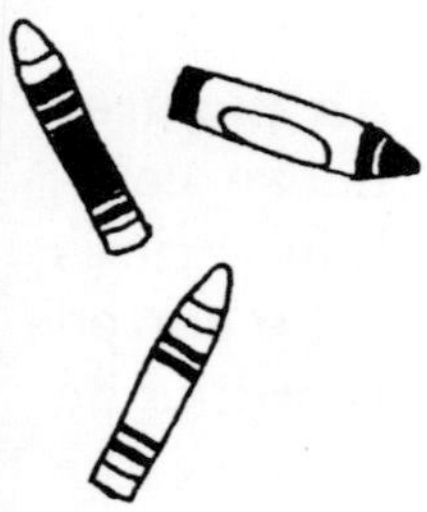

WHAT ARE APPROPRIATE ART ACTIVITIES FOR YOUNG CHILDREN?

Art activities encourage young children to explore their own creativity. You will observe that when children are offered art opportunities the process of creating is as important as the actual finished product.

ART ACTIVITIES: A FEW IMPORTANT GUIDELINES

- Some art activity should be available each day.
  - cutting, gluing, drawing or coloring
- **Consider how many and what type of art activities you can supervise in any given day.**
- **Start your art program with simple art materials.**
  - **i.e., large crayons, flow pens, paper and pencil. Add scissors glue, paints, chalk and clay materials at a later time.**

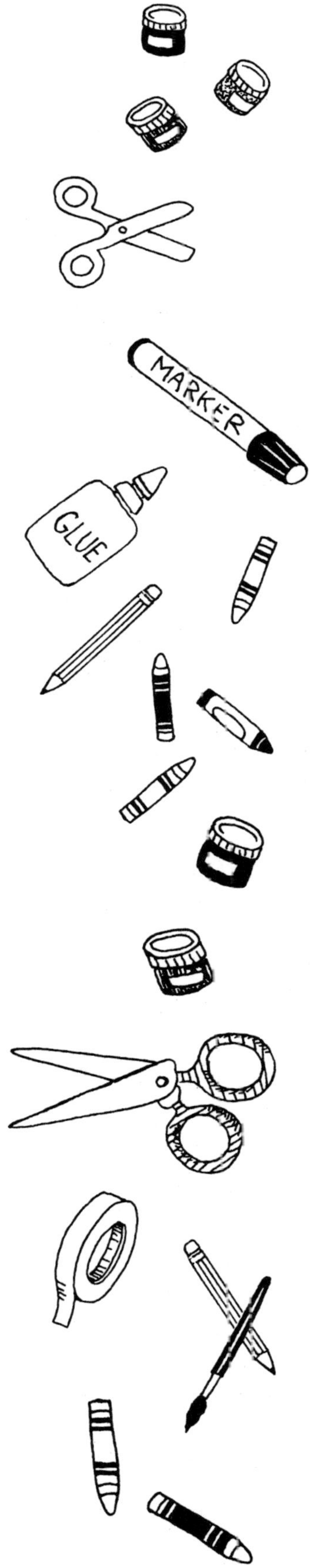

- Prepare and present the materials to the children, but allow the children to do all the work themselves.
- Create clear rules on **how** and **where** to use art materials.
- Allowing children to express themselves freely with the materials does not mean they can use materials to create a mess or destroy things.
- Encourage children to explore, experiment and use their own ideas. **Avoid using patterns.**
- Present messy art activities, such as painting, finger painting or clay, when you are free to supervise and have time for the preparation of these materials.
- **Painting and messy art activities can happen outside.**
- **Use drop cloths, newspapers, or other coverings to protect floors and walls.**
- **Have a pail of water, sponges and paper towels available so children can assist with the cleanup.**
- **The art area should:**
  - **Have good lighting, and natural light if possible.**
  - **Be close to a source of water, if water is needed.**
  - **Not interfere with other activities in the room.**
  - **Have enough room for 3-4 children at a time.**
  - **Not be difficult for children or you to clean.**
  - **Be away from unprotected furniture.**
  - **Have a place for children's things to dry and for finished art work.**

Remember, children are eager to help in the set up and cleanup of art activities if they know you depend on their help and their cooperation.

GROUND RULES FOR CHILDREN

1. All materials must be handled with care and supervised at all times.
2. Art materials must not be wasted, spilled, thrown or destroyed.
3. Children cannot put paste, glue, paint, chalk or other materials into their mouths.
4. Art materials are to be kept in the art area.
5. Painting and other messy activities are only to be done in a special place with supervision.
6. Children cannot paint on themselves or others.

TIPS FOR SETTING UP A PAINTING ACTIVITY

1. Provide aprons or old adult t-shirts to protect the children's clothing.
2. Use thicker paint and wider brushes with younger children.
3. Use two or three primary colors for beginners.
4. Avoid asking children what they are painting.
5. Allow them to touch and smear the paint.
6. Adding detergent to paint can make cleaning up easier.

PAINTING ACTIVITIES

SUGGESTED ART RECIPES

EASEL PAINT

#1. Fill a 3 oz. juice can about ⅓ full of powdered tempera. Stir in about 4 tbls. liquid starch. Thin to desired consistency with water.

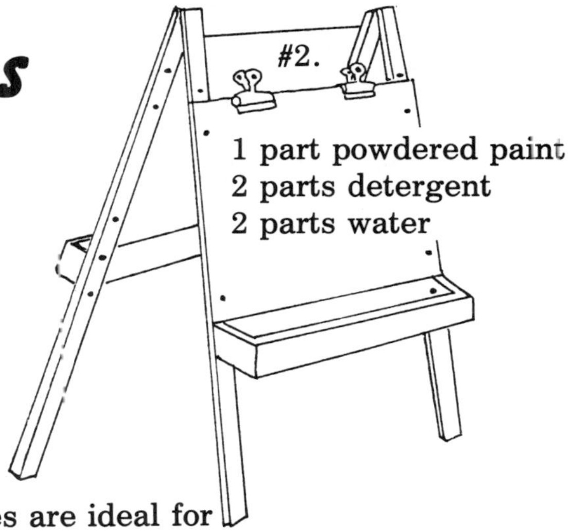

- Buckets or cans of water and large paint brushes are ideal for "painting" back fences and the outsides of houses.

FINGER PAINTS

Add a non-detergent liquid soap to liquid starch to facilitate cleanup. Sprinkle powdered tempera on top of starch as used.

THINGS TO DO WITH PAINT

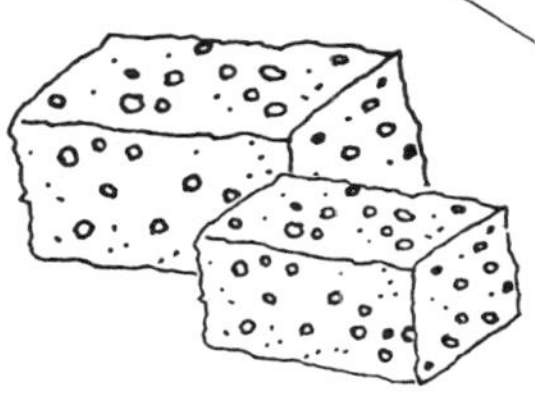

- Some caregivers let children fingerpaint on old cafeteria trays, and then make a print by patting a piece of paper over the design and lifting it slowly back up. With this method the paint on the tray can be reused by many children.

- EXPERIMENT WITH: sponges, cotton balls, ice cream sticks, leaves, string, sand, coffee grounds, and other textured materials.
- MAKE PRINTED PATTERNS by cutting vegetables, and dipping them first into the paint, and then onto the paper. Try using a carrot, or cutting a potato half into a shape.

- PAINT ON MATERIALS LIKE: cardboard boxes, egg cartons, wood scraps. Detergent added to paint will help it to adhere to glass, metal, plastic and aluminum foil.

- FOR A STAINED GLASS EFFECT ON PAPER TOWELS: Fill cups in muffin tin with 5 drops of food coloring diluted in a bit of water. Let toddlers dip folded or wadded paper towels into the colors. Unfold and hang near a window to dry.

PLAY-DOH

Play-doh is a homemade play clay which will not hurt children if they put it in their mouths. You and the children can choose and change the color of the dough by adding a few drops of food coloring.

This cooked version of play-doh is a teacher's favorite. Not only does it last longer and feel better than other doughs, but you can give it to the children while it is still warm, to roll and pound and shape.

#1. **Cooked Play-doh**
3 cups flour
1 cup salt
3 cups water
(add food coloring)
4 tbls vegetable oil
2 tbls cream of tartar
(from spice section at the store)

Blend, and cook over low heat. Stir to consistency of mashed potatoes. Store in tightly covered container up to 3 weeks.

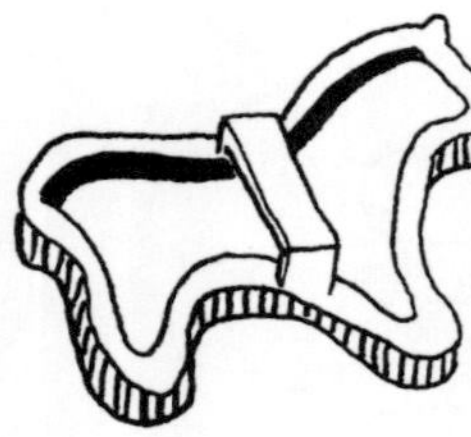

#2. **Play-doh (uncooked version)**
2 cups flour
1 cup salt
1 cup warm water
(add food coloring)

Mix flour and salt. Slowly stir in liquid to kneading consistency. Add 2 drops oil, stir.
Note: Store in a plastic bag in refrigerator. To re-use, roll in flour.

Remember that you can add cookie cutters, a rolling pin, dull knives, etc. to the dough as children become increasingly skilled at manipulating it.

BAKERS CLAY

This dough is similar to play-doh in texture but may be baked in oven for hardened pieces. These make excellent Christmas ornaments; a hairpin inserted while soft will bake into clay as a hanger.

4 cups flour
1 cup salt
1½ cups water

Knead dough until soft. Shape as desired. Bake finished pieces for 1 hour or until hardened. They can be painted afterwards.

SOAP FLAKES MODELING

For a different "dough" with minimal cleanup, try mixing:
2 cups soap flakes + ¼ cup water.
Mix together until dough can be modeled into shapes.
Let dry for two days.

COLLAGE ACTIVITIES

Collect items such as feathers, seed pods, shells, buttons, ribbon, magazine pictures, yarn and wrapping paper. Let children make ''feeling'' pictures with rough and smooth textures. Let the children use glue (paste tends to be eaten), in plastic squeeze containers. (Plastic catsup bottles become good glue containers).

#1. Tissue Collage
Let children use wide brushes to ''paint'' liquid starch on cardboard tubes, cans, construction paper, etc. and apply pieces of colored tissue paper. Let dry, and hang for display.

#2. Window Transparency
Let children make a design on a sheet of wax paper by placing colored tissues, leaves, scrapped bits of old crayons and other flat materials. Cover with similar size paper and iron together. Hang in window for transparency.

#3. Easy Stained Glass
With toddlers, turn a piece of contact paper sticky side up and let them press on pieces of yarn, pictures, papers, etc. Place a second piece of contact paper over it for a see-through effect.

DRAWING ACTIVITIES

Crayons and paper should be readily available for the children. Remember that art activities do not have to be complicated. They are for the children, not for the adults. Thus art activities, like other learning activities, should be age appropriate and encourage creativity and discovery.

The following ideas are for those days when both you and the children want to add another dimension to their usual drawing time.

#1. TEXTURED RUBBINGS:
Place paper over leaves, ferns, tree bark, then lightly rub the side of a peeled crayon over the textured pattern.

#2. SIDEWALK DRAWING:
Large chalk can be used on concrete walkways, and backyards for drawing larger pictures (it can also be hosed off if desired).

Remember: Drawing materials such as chalk, crayons, watercolor felt tip pens and a variety of paper, should be kept readily available for the older children. Scissors and glue can also be available. Youngsters enjoy experimenting with shape and color. You can help the children understand that their creations need only please them, and that you will help only if needed.

WHAT ARE APPROPRIATE MUSIC ACTIVITIES FOR YOUNG CHILDREN?

Young children move, sing, dance, tap, chat, hum, drum, etc., with grace and great enjoyment. You can encourage their natural enthusiasm by offering a variety of musical activities on a daily basis.

- Try making a list of songs you already know, and add new ones slowly.
- Play children's records and tapes.
- Invest in rhythm instruments like tambourines, bells and maracas for the children to use.
- Take children to listen to live music, or invite musicians to come to play for the children.
- Older children enjoy listening to popular music. Occasionally turn the radio to their favorite stations.
- Keep music volume at a level that does not override normal conversation.
- Try classical music at nap time for a soothing affect.

A music program is almost always successful in proportion to the amount of enthusiasm the adult brings to it. If you like music, the children will like it too. Here are a few songs and fingerplays you can use in your program. Remember to keep things simple and have fun.

IF YOU'RE HAPPY AND YOU KNOW IT, CLAP YOUR HANDS

If you're happy and you know it,
clap your hands.
If you're happy and you know it,
clap your hands.
If you're happy and you know it,
then your face will clearly show it.
If you're happy and you know it,
clap your hands.

other verses ...tap your foot
...rub your tummy
...wave your arms

RING AROUND THE ROSES

Ring around the roses,
Pockets full of posies,
Ashes, ashes
We all fall down!
(circle, holding hands, fall down)

(KAZOO)

OLD MAC DONALD

Old Mc Donald had a farm, EI, EI, OH.
And on his farm he had some chicks,
EI, EI, OH.
With a chick, chick here, And a chick, chick, there.
Here a chick, there a chick
Everywhere a chick, chick
Old McDonald had a farm, EI, EI, OH.

EENSY WEENSY SPIDER

The eensy weensy spider crawled up the water spout.
(fingers creep upward)
Down came the rain
(fingers flutter down)
And washed the spider out.
(sweeping out motion with arms)
Out came the sun and dried up all the rain;
(make a sun with arms overhead)
So the eensy weensy spider crawled up the spout again.
(fingers creep up)

Vary the song by singing the great, big hairy spider. Lower the pitch of your voice and enlarge the finger play to indicate a large spider.

TWINKLE, TWINKLE

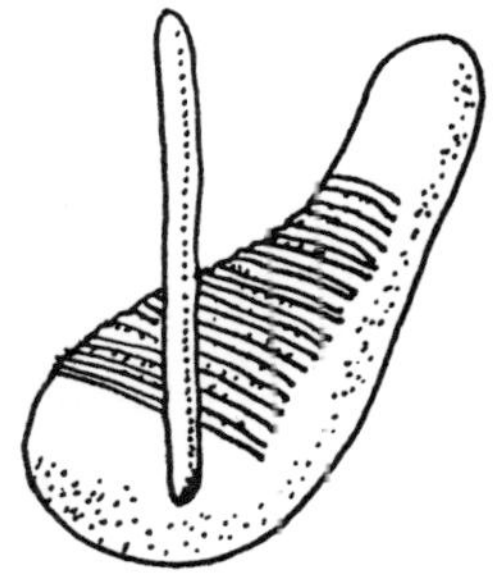

Twinkle, twinkle little star
How I wonder what you are
Up above the world so high
Like a Diamond in the sky
I wish I may I wish I might
Have the wish I wish tonight.

WHERE IS THUMBKIN?

(To the tune of Frere Jacques or your own tune)

Where is thumbkin? **(keep fists, thumbs up,**
Where is thumbkin? **behind back)**
Here I am! **(bring one hand, then**
Here I am! **the other to front)**
How are you today, sir? **(raise and lower thumbs**
Very well, I thank you. **to mime a conversation)**
Run away. **(put one hand, then the**
Run away. **other, behind back)**

Each finger can play a part. First finger is Pointer. Second finger is Tall Man. Third finger is Ring Man. Little finger is Pinky.

Toddler Record List

Music For One's and Two's	Tom Glazer (CMS Records)
Let's Sing Fingerplays	Tom Glazer (CMS Records)
Whoever Shall Have Some Good Peanuts	Sam Hinton
Creative Movement and Rhythmic Expression	Hap Palmer (Activity Records)
Homemade Band Activity Record	Hap Palmer (Activity Records)
You'll Sing a Song and I'll Sing a Song	Ella Jenkins (Folkways)
Burl Ives Sings Little White Duck	Burl Ives (Columbia)
Mother Goose	Cyril Richard, Celeste Holm, Boris Karloff (Caedmon)
Golden Slumbers-Lullabies from Near & Far	with Pete Seeger (Caedmon)
Sing the Hit Songs of Sesame St.	(Children's Records of America)
Anne Murray Sings for the Sesame St. Generation	(Sesame St. Records)
Spin, Spider, Spin	Patty Zeitlin, Marcia Berman (Educational Activities, Inc.)
Marches	Arthur Fiedler and the Boston Pops Orchestra (Time Life Records)
Abiyoyo	Pete Seeger (Folkways)

IS IT A GOOD IDEA TO READ BOOKS TO YOUNG CHILDREN EVEN BEFORE THEY CAN READ?

Yes, most definitely! Reading to young children provides both of you with a private moment, a moment of intimacy when you can snuggle and giggle and play. It is a relaxing fun activity that also introduces the child into the world of books. If children can associate books with pleasurable experiences they are most likely to want to continue reading beyond the days when you hold them on your lap.

Reading to a child also develops good communication skills and helps in building a child's vocabulary. Sounding out each word carefully, and mimicking each other are all fun ways to assist a child in developing speech.

Reading also encourages adults to act out the child in themselves and provides both children and adults with an opportunity to learn about each other's world.

TIPS FOR READING WITH CHILDREN

1. Choose books carefully to suit child's interest and age.
2. Read new books first to yourself. You will be a better reader with the children.
3. Find a regular quiet time to read every day.
4. Let children help pick out books to be read.
5. Use your hands and voice to dramatize a story.
6. Explain the text, when necessary, in whispered asides.
7. Never force a child to read with you.

The following list are suggested titles. Visit your library on a regular basis, and offer stories to the children every day.

Ask Mr. Bear .... Marjorie Flack
Best Word Book Ever .... Richard Scarry
Cars and Trucks and Things That Go .... Golden Press
Baby Farm Animals .... Golden Press
Goodnight Moon .... Margaret Wise Brown
The Snowy Day .... Ezra Jack Keats
A Boy, A Dog and A Frog .... Mercer Mayer
Whistle For Willie .... Ezra Jack Keats
Goggles .... Ezra Jack Keats

Corduroy .... Don Freeman
One fish, two fish, red fish, blue fish .... Dr. Seuss
Where The Wild Things Are .... Maurice Sendak
Noise In The Night .... Anne Alexander
Sleepy Time .... Gyo Fujikawa
Pat The Bunny .... Dorothy Kunhardt
The Noisy Book .... Margaret Wise Brown
The Little Rabbit Who Wanted Red Wings .... Carolyn Sherwin Bailey
That's What Friends Are For .... Frances Heide and Sylvia Van Clief
Ferdinand .... Munro Leaf

A Letter To Amy .... Ezra Jack Keats
Gilberto and The Wind .... Marie Hall Ets
Amigo .... Byed Boyou Schweitzer
The Story About Ping .... Marjorie Flack
Blueberries For Sal .... Robert McCloskey
Brian WildSmith's ABC .... Brian WildSmith
Rosie's Walk .... Pat Hutchins
Inch By Inch .... Leo Lionni
Make Way For Ducklings .... Robert McClosky
Peter's Chair .... Ezra Jack Keats
When My Father Was A Little Boy .... Jay Lonergon
Stone Soup .... Marcia Brown

HOW CAN I HELP CHILDREN WITH THEIR SPEECH?

Some children will begin talking long before others of the same age. This emphasizes what caregivers have observed: each child is an individual, developing skills at his or her own pace.

If you are already listening and talking to the children, you are carrying out the basic principles of language stimulation. Here are some suggestions to use to help children develop speech at their own rates.

INFANTS:

- Feeding, bathing and diaper changing times can be used to exchange coos and gurgles. Eye contact, listening, laughing and experimenting with sounds are key.

TODDLERS:

- Saying the names of items as you use them, describing what you are doing and always listening can help the rapid rate of speech development now.
  - Keep it simple
  - Speak naturally—avoid baby talk
  - Give children time to answer
  - Listen to them speak

PRESCHOOLERS:

- These children can hardly get enough of the books, songs, stories, imitation and repetition that have been referred to in other chapters.
  - Allow children time to put their thoughts into words.
  - Allow some speech mistakes as children learn.

  - Don't ask them to slow down or repeat what they have said.
  - Keep interruptions to a minimum.

  - Expand their vocabulary by offering more words.

"Give doggie dinner?"
"Yes, I'm giving the dog his dinner."

SCHOOL-AGE:

- Children's understanding and use of language are tools they have for learning in school and in the world around them. Just as they will explore their environment, let them explore and discover the exciting world of language.
  - Exchange ideas, stories and experiences with them.
  - Give them time to explain and describe events and feelings.

  - Answer questions and satisfy their natural curiosity.
  - Ask questions to stimulate their interests.
  - Encourage them to put their thoughts and stories on paper.

CAUTION

Before children produce their own speech they must be able to hear and understand what other people are saying. If you have to repeat phrases frequently or talk loudly to a particular child, let the parents know. Urge them to seek professional help if you are concerned about a hearing or speech problem.

Don't wait for someone else to spot the problem. Your sensitivity as a care-giver can be valuable for an early referral if necessary. Professional help is available and effective at an early stage.

Resources are:

- Your local Easter Seal Society
- University based speech, language and hearing clinics
- Public school speech and hearing screening programs
- Audiologists
- Speech Pathologists

HEARING AND UNDERSTANDING		TALKING
- Startles or cries at sudden sounds - Awakens to loud noises - Appears to respond to speaker	**0 to 3 months**	- Cries when uncomfortable - Coos and gurgles when content
- Turns her head to sounds - Disturbed by angry voices - Stops crying with soothing words or a familiar voice - Interrupts activity to listen	**3 to 6 months**	- Plays with making sounds - Has a special cry for hunger - Laughs when played with - Has a variety of sounds - Babbles by repeating series of same sound "ma-ma-ma-ma"
- Looks for source of sounds or music - Responds to "no" and her name - Distinguishes happy or angry voices - Appears to recognize a few words (bye-bye, mama, up, no, ball)	**6 to 10 months**	- Babbles in response to speaker - Appears to be imitating - Babbling develops sentence-like rhythms - May attempt to sing along - Uses gestures and facial expressions with speech sounds
- Turns or looks up when called - Uses hand and body movements in rhythm to music - Listens to and responds to some spoken requests - Shows interest in new words	**10 to 12 months**	- First words may be heard - Uses speech and gestures games (pat-a-cake, peek-a-boo) - Tries to imitate - "Talks" to toys and people in long patterns
- Recognizes names of parts of her body, clothing, toys - Looks at or points to pictures named in books - May follow two instructions	**12 to 20 months**	- Uses true words, gestures and jargon - Asks or repeats questions - Vocabulary may grow from 2 to 20 words - Imitates the sounds of toys, motors, animals
- Understands new words daily including size, shape, and relationships - Distinguishes different sounds (knock at door, dog barking, telephone ringing) - Hears television at the same sound level as the group does - Comes or hides when you call from another room	**2 to 3 years**	- Begins combining words to form short sentences - Asks for "food," "toilet," "outside," etc. - Uses some pronouns, "me" - Tells immediate experiences with words and jargon
- Interested in explanations of how and why - Hears and understands long stories - Carries out 3 simple spoken instructions	**3 to 4 years**	- Jargon decreases, and disappears - Asks "why" questions - Forms short sentences - Grammatical structures increase - Uses sounds in their right places
- Listens for long periods of time - Understands conversation	**5 years**	- Tells stories haltingly - Engages in conversation - Almost all sounds are present

WHAT IS THE PURPOSE OF PROVIDING MULTI-CULTURAL EXPERIENCES FOR YOUNG CHILDREN?

The feelings of pride in one's own lifestyle and one's own way of thinking are a powerful influence in helping children view themselves as worthwhile and valued human beings. Caregivers have a responsibility to model positive attitudes toward all people. A provider must feel good about her/himself and what he/she is doing in order to be an effective role model for children and to encourage them to feel good about themselves. A child's first idea of her/himself as a person depends upon the responses of others. As caregivers you are in a position to provide support to parent(s) while they are educating their young children about who they are and how they relate to their community, their city and country.

There are significant reasons why providing multi-cultural experiences for young children is important.

1. To make children feel good about who they are irrespective of their nationality, race, gender or ability.
2. To share cultural diversity with other children so that they may respect and appreciate cultures different from their own.

A positive ethnic identity (secondary identity) must be built on an inner core of pride and positive feelings (primary identity). As a caregiver, you understand the importance of building a positive inner and outer self image in the young child's development.

Race is a complicated concept which children learn over time. There is little or no interest in the question of skin color or racial variation until about three years of age.

You can discuss color and race related issues in a natural way with the children in your care. For example, you can talk about characteristics of the body to children in a way that includes skin color and hair. It must be presented in a way that makes the children feel good about themselves. For example, *"The color of your skin is black, black is a very pretty color. Have you ever heard the saying, 'black is beautiful,' or 'I'm black and I'm proud'?"*

Multi-cultural diversity can be shared in your reading materials, pictures that may be displayed on your walls, field trips that you plan for your children, activities and games played at the site. Most importantly cultural values will be shared in your attitudes towards other races and cultures.

The following is a list of suggestions to help make your home culturally diverse:

1. Make reference to and plan a curriculum around special ethnic holidays like Kwanza, Hanukkah, Black History Month, Chinese New Years, etc.

2. When possible, include in your curriculum facts about famous people of color, such as Black poet Phyllis Wheatley or Puerto Rican ball player Roberto Clemente.

3. When you read stories to the children, include stories by and about Black cultures, Spanish-speaking cultures, Asian and Native American cultures. Be sensitive and alert to books that may be culturally offensive. Avoid books that stereotype people of color, gender or ability or ones in which they are depicted as being poor, troublemakers, from broken families or stupid.

When possible, include folk tales and audio-visual materials.

4. Utilize your closest resources: the children, parents and grandparents. Ask if the children have any material at home to share that might offer cultural diversity. Have them ask their parents and grandparents to share some part of living history. Ask the parents to share artifacts and information that they may have about other cultures. Grandparents are great storytellers.

5. You may ask a parent to prepare an ethnic lunch for you or give you a recipe for an ethnic lunch or snack. Why not eat a meal with chopsticks? (One parent suggested a way to make using chopsticks easier for the little ones. Try placing a small, folded piece of paper between the two chopsticks, and then wrapping them with a rubber band. This way, the paper acts as a spacer, and the rubber band holds the chopsticks together).

6. During music time play culturally diverse music, like Latin, Asian, classical, soul, etc. If you have the luxury of being able to buy musical instruments, be selective and include instruments of various cultures. Maybe you can find a musical group that uses steel drums that play for children and that will allow them to touch and experiment with their instruments.

7. Many cultural groups offer free guest speakers and entertainers to come to your site. Why not invite another family day caregiver who may live close by?

8. Pictures that you have displayed on you wall should include people of different cultures. If possible avoid stereotyped pictures, like a black child that has all white characteristics or girls doing "traditionally female" activities.

9. Some areas are very rich in cultural diversity. Utilize those resources. If you live in an urban area and you have preschoolers, take them on a trip to Japantown, Chinatown, or the Afro-American historical and cultural society.

10. Your public library has a wealth of information. You can start by borrowing library books. They may also loan you records, pictures, tapes and video cassettes.

11. Why not learn words from another language? It is easy to learn how to count from one to ten in Spanish, for example.

12. Show people of different cultures and genders in everyday activities.

SUGGESTED BOOKS FOR CHILDREN

BLACK CULTURES
Ashanti to Zulu
The Black Snowman
The Chalk Doll
Children of Long Ago
Darkness and the Butterfly
Daydreamers
Everett Anderson's Goodbye
Follow the Drinking Gourd
Galimoto
Grandmama's Joy
Grandpa's Face
Honey, I Love
Jamaica's Find
Martin Luther King, Jr.: A Biography for Young Children
Mufaro's Beautiful Daughters
Nathaniel Talking
Osa's Pride
A Rose for Abbey
Something on My Mind
The Talking Eggs
The Train to Lulu's
Under the Sunday Tree
The Village of Round and Square Houses

SPANISH-SPEAKING CULTURES
The Adventures of Connie and Diego/Las aventuras de Connie y Diego (Bilingual)
Alexander y el dia terrible, horrible, espantoso, horroroso (Spanish Edition)
Are You My Mother? (Bilingual)
Arroz con leche: Popular Songs and Rhymes from Latin America (Bilingual)
Atariba y Niguayona (Bilingual)
Buenas Noches, Luna (Spanish Edition)
Corduroy (Spanish Edition)
Family Pictures (Bilingual)
Friday Night Is Papa Night
Gilberto and the Wind
The Invisible Hunters/ Los cazadores invisibles (Bilingual)
My House/Mi Casa (Bilingual)
La oruga muy hambrienta (Spanish Edition)
Las navidades (Bilingual)
Mr. Sugar Came to Town/La visita del Sr. Azucar (Bilingual)
Taking a Walk/Caminando (Bilingual)
Uncle Nacho's Hat/El sombrero del tio Nacho (Bilingual)

ASIAN CULTURES
Aekyung's Dream
Angel Child, Dragon Child
The Empty Pot
How the Ox Star Fell From Heaven
The Magic Boat
Nine-In-One Grr! Grr!
Our Home Is the Sea
Sachiko Means Happpiness
Toad Is the Uncle of Heaven
The Story About Ping
The Tears of the Dragon

NATIVE AMERICAN CULTURES
Baby Rattlesnake
Beyond the Ridge
The Flute Player
The Friendly Wolf
The Girl Who Loved Wild Horses
The Legend of the Blue Bonnet
The Legend of the Indian Paintbrush
Lone Bull's Horse Raid
Mud Pony
North American Indians
Red Hawk's Account of Custer's Last Battle

MULTICULTURAL BOOKS
All About Things People Do
All Kinds of Families
The Big Book for Peace
Bread, Bread, Bread
The Day of Ahmed's Secret
Everybody Cooks Rice
Granny Will Your Dog Bite?
Hats, Hats, Hats,
Here Are My Hands
Here Comes the Cat
Loving
Potluck
The Relatives Came
School Picnic
Thunder Cake
Uncle Vova's Tree
When I Was Young in the Mountains

REFERENCES

Blackie, J. *Inside the Primary School.* London: Her Majesty's Stationery Office, 1967.

Cherry, C. *Creative Art for the Developing Child.* Belmont, CA: Fearon Publishing, 1972.

Elkind, D. *The Hurried Child.* Menlo Park, CA: Addison Wesley, 1983.

Gellert, S., Hollestelle, K., and Kotlus, E. & The Equity Project Team; *Helping Children Love Themselves and Others: A Professional Handbook for Family Day Care,* Washington, D.C., The Children's Foundation, 1990.

Gerber, M. *Resources for Infant Educarers,* Los Angeles, CA: 1550 Murray Circle, 90026, 1981.

Jones, E. *Supporting the Growth of Infants, Toddlers and Parents.* Pasadena, CA: Pacific Oaks College, 1979.

Lally, J.R. and Gordon, I. *Learning Games for Infant and Toddlers.* Syracuse, NY: Non Readers Press, 1977.

Millar, S. *The Psychology of Play.* Maryland: Penguin Books, 1968.

Piaget, J. and Inhelder, B. *The Psychology of the Child.* New York: Basic Books, 1969.

Pickler, E. ''Some Contributions to the Study of the Gross Motor Development of Children''. *Journal of Genetic Psychology.* (1968) Vol. 3, 27-39.

Sponsellor, D., ed. *Play As a Learning Medium.* Washington, D.C.: National Association for the Education of Young Children, 1974.

Section V

STANDARDS FOR QUALITY CARE

Chapter 11

ACCIDENT PREVENTION AND FIRST AID

Designing a safe environment which provides a minimum of restrictions, and which encourages children to move and explore freely is a challenging proposition. We know that children do fall and hurt themselves during the normal process of growing up. Children who are constantly restricted and kept from falling are prevented from learning about their bodies and thus may have the accident you wanted to avoid.

Children learn through their experiences, and practice and experimentation are the keys to this learning. But be aware of the dangers surrounding most play situations.

Today, accidents loom as the nation's number one threat to all children and are a serious menace to infants. Choking, suffocation, automobile accidents, fires and falls cause a great many infant deaths. Children from 1 to 4 years are menaced by motor vehicle accidents, fires and drowning. They are also frequent poisoning victims, especially at age one.

Accidents can be prevented, and emergencies can be handled. This chapter outlines ways you can work to prevent accidents from occurring in your family day care home. Many caregivers make it a practice to review a safety checklist for their homes on a regular basis. You may consider trading checklists with other caregivers in your community and evaluating each other's homes for safety.

Each state has different guidelines to follow for licensing or registration. The checklist below is used in some communities as a basic outline of minimal requirements.

- ☐ Smoke Detectors and Fire Extinguisher
- ☐ First Aid Kit
- ☐ Gates across stairs (both inside and out and top and bottom)
- ☐ Poisons, Detergents and Medicines stored in locked cabinets
- ☐ Gate to kitchen and lock-clips on drawers and cabinets where children can reach
- ☐ Emergency phone numbers posted near telephone, including medical, police, parents, poison control, fire department
- ☐ Diaper changing pad which can be wiped off after each use with a bleach solution
- ☐ Heaters and Fireplaces must be screened

However, quality caregiving environments require more than the minimum. Guidelines for structuring safety into all rooms requires a combination of common sense and a knowledge of how children grow and develop at different ages.

- Get to know each child's physical skills, and remember these skills change daily.

- Don't lift children onto any equipment or surface they cannot climb on themselves. Instead, observe how they choose to get on the equipment. For example, toddlers usually choose to climb up the slope of the slide before they choose to climb up the ladder. They usually choose to climb back down the ladder before they choose to come down the slide.

- When children fall down, your first reaction may be to pick them up. If the fall is not serious, try not to overreact. Instead, wait and see how they behave. If they are seriously hurt, their cry and hesitancy to move will indicate that they need your help. Otherwise, most youngster recover quickly, and appreciate your acknowledgement of their heightened abilities.

KITCHEN

The heart of any home is the kitchen. Children are likely to be with you at times while you are preparing food or fetching the ever popular drink of water. Unfortunately this room with all its cupboards, shelves, counters and assortment of appliances is a household collection of potential danger signs.

There are specific steps to take to make your kitchen a safe environment.

- Knives, poisons and matches are best kept high above the reach of children and behind locked doors.
- Cabinets and drawers can be locked with store bought safety latches or secured with stretch ties, rubber bands or strong fasteners.

- Eliminate accidental scalding by setting your water heater at a low temperature (120 degrees).
- Prevent falls in the kitchen by wiping up spills and grease immediately. Be sure area rugs are slip resistant.

- Limit running and roughhousing in this room.
- Never keep an unused refrigerator or freezer anywhere in your home unless the door is removed or sealed shut so a child cannot get inside.
- Never leave young children alone in the kitchen.

LIVING ROOM—DINING ROOM: These are often the rooms caregivers decide to use for the children's play activities. They are also the rooms most likely to have been decorated.

- It is a good idea to remove all items that can be dangerous, or easily broken by children. All glass items and decorations which can be pulled over by children should be removed during operating hours. This includes:
  - glass coffee tables and ash trays
  - statues, figurines and photographs
  - valuable books and other family treasures

- Fireplaces and heaters should be covered or screened at all times. Matches, smoking items, and ashtrays should be kept out of children's sight and reach.

- TV and VCR and stereo equipment is expensive and fragile. To avoid damage, place these items in areas away from play spaces.

- Tablecloths can be tempting items for children to pull. Placemats may be an alternative.

- Be sure your household and garden plants are not poisonous (many are). Your community poison control center, listed in the telephone directory, will send you free information about child-proofing your home.

- Unused electrical outlets should be covered with safety covers. Electrical cords should be pulled back, hidden behind furniture and out of reach. Remember that crawling infants can accidentally pull a heavy lamp or appliance over on themselves by grasping a cord.

BEDROOMS AND BATHROOMS:

- Adult bedrooms are the second leading site of poisoning accidents. Be especially careful about cosmetics and medicines.

  - Keep medicines, perfumes and cosmetics out of reach. Children are often left alone in this room during nap time, so double check it on a daily basis for hidden dangers.

  - The plastic coverings on clothing from the dry cleaners can be extremely dangerous. Be careful to dispose of them safely.

- Do not use plastic bags to store toys or diapers, or as liners for cribs or mattresses.

- Never leave a small child alone in a tub or sink, or on a changing table. Prepare for these routines prior to beginning the caregiving activity. (See Chapter 1 for details).

- Keep unused rooms latched. These rooms may include the laundry, garage, den or other bedrooms.

- Supervise the children at all times.

Knowing that you have done all you can to prevent accidents can be reassuring. But being prepared in case of an accident can save a life!

It is not the purpose of this book to be used as a first aid manual. In the case of an accident you should be reaching for your first aid kit which contains a first aid handbook like the ones listed at the end of this section.

When an emergency strikes, knowing what to do while reacting **quickly and calmly** before medical help arrives will enable you to provide the best care possible for the victim, whether it be yourself or one of the children.

Taking a first aid class and an infant CPR class offered in your community before the accident occurs is a common sense approach to anticipating accidents and knowing how to respond.

When And Where To Call For Help:

- If the injured child is in distress but is breathing, phone for help at once. Notify the parents immediately.

- If the injured child is not breathing, offer help first, and phone later, or get someone else to phone. Notify parents immediately.

- When making an emergency call:
  - Ask for the fire department or paramedics.
  - State clearly and slowly the nature of the emergency.
  - Give your name, address and phone number.
  - Do not hang up. Stay on the phone to answer additional questions or give directions.

What To Have In Your First Aid Kit:

- Box of assorted bandages
- Scissors and tweezers
- Absorbent cotton
- Anti-bacterial soap
- Roll of 1-inch adhesive tape
- Hydrogen peroxide (to clean cuts, bites)
- Child's rectal thermometer
- Petroleum jelly
- Safety pins
- 3-inch sterile gauze squares
- Rolls of 1 and 2 inch sterile gauze
- Baby tylenol or aspirin substitute
- Syrup of ipecac (to induce vomiting)
- A First Aid Handbook

Be sure to keep the kit well out of the reach of children.

BEE STINGS:

(1) If stung by a bee, carefully remove the stinger.

(2) Wash the area with soap.

(3) Place ice wrapped in cloth or cold compresses on sting area to decrease absorption and spread of the venom.

(4) Soothing lotions such as calamine or a paste of baking soda and a little water are often helpful in relieving discomfort.

(5) Notify the child's parent(s).

CHOKING:

(1) If the child can cry, speak, cough or breath, do not interfere in any way with the child's efforts to cough out a swallowed or partially swallowed object.

(2) If the child cannot breathe, position yourself slightly to one side of her and support her chest with one hand. With the heel of the other hand give four quick, forceful blows on the back between her shoulder blades.

(3) Be sure you have taken an annual first aid class to become knowledgeable of other procedures.

(4) Depending on severity, notify child's parent(s).

BURNS:

The objectives of first aid for burns are to relieve pain, prevent infection and prevent or treat for shock.

Burns caused by fire, sunlight or hot substances are classified according to the degree of the injury—first-degree burns being the least dangerous, third-degree burns the most.

FIRST-DEGREE BURNS:

(1) Immediately put burned area under cold running water or apply cold-water compress (clean towel, washcloth, handkerchief, etc.) until pain decreases.

(2) Notify the child's parent(s).

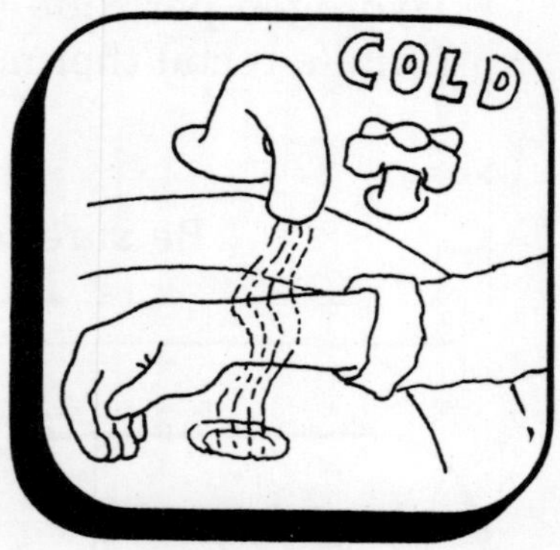

SECOND-DEGREE BURNS:

(1) If you observe blisters, blotchy appearance or swelling, put burned area in cold water (not iced) or apply cold-water compress until pain subsides. Gently pay dry.

(2) Cover burned area with a dry sterile bandage to prevent infection, and seek medical attention.

(3) Notify the child's parent(s).

THIRD-DEGREE BURNS:

You may observe that the burned area looks white or charred, the skin destroyed, or that little pain is present because the nerve endings have been destroyed.

(1) Call for an ambulance immediately. It is very important that victims with even small third-degree burns consult a doctor.

- Do not remove clothes that are stuck to the burn.
- **Do not put ice or ice water on burns**. This can intensify shock reactions.
- Do not apply ointments, sprays, antiseptics or home remedies to burns.

(2) Place cold cloth or cool water (not iced) on burns.

(3) Consult your first aid book, and treat for shock.

(4) Notify the child's parent(s).

POISONING From Household Products That Have Been Swallowed:

(1) Telephone your community Poison Control Center, hospital emergency room, or the fire department for instructions if someone has swallowed a poison. Be prepared to give the child's age, name of poison, how much poison was swallowed and whether or not the child has vomited.

(2) Do not induce vomiting if you do not know what the child has swallowed. Acids and petroleum products, such as gasoline and furniture polish, may cause further damage to the throat if vomiting is induced.

(3) Never give liquid to dilute the poison or induce vomiting if the victim is unconscious or is having convulsions.

(4) Follow medical advice to dilute poison with water or milk. Do not give fruit juice or vinegar to neutralize the poison.

(5) Notify the child's parent(s).

FEVER:

(1) Report any fever over 101 degrees to parent(s).

(2) Keep the child calm, and encourage her to drink fluids (unless vomiting).

(3) For fevers over 101 degrees consult parent(s) for medical management.

- There are fever reducing medications which are effective. However, research is finding a connection between fevers treated with aspirin and Reye's Syndrome. Alternatives to aspirins are acetaminophen drugs like tylenol.

CONVULSIONS:

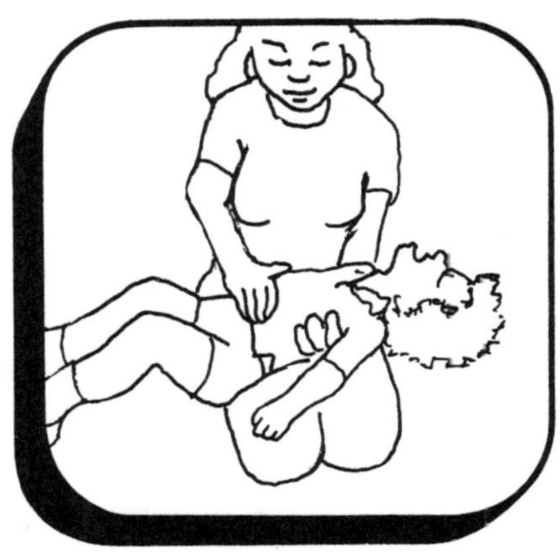

Convulsions in young children are not uncommon. The most frequent cause is rapid rise in temperature due to an infection, usually when the child is under three years and has a history of convulsions.

(1) Do not panic. Make sure the child is comfortable.

(2) Maintain an open airway. Tip head back, and check to make sure that the child's tongue is not blocking her throat.

(3) After the convulsions pass, contact the child's physician or an ambulance for immediate treatment.

(4) Notify the child's parent(s).

From *The American Medical Associations Handbook of First Aid And Emergency Care,* Random House, 1980.

Chapter 12

IN SICKNESS AND IN HEALTH

The average child has 6 to 8 colds a year, lasting from 7 to 10 days. It is inevitable that there are times when a sick child will be in your group. Excluding all children with colds from your program may be disruptive for both the children and their parents.

You have a unique relationship with the families, and an insight into the complexities of their personal circumstances. Family day care offers an opportunity to respond to minor illnesses while being sensitive to the individual needs (job, school, stress) of families. But as a caregiver, you also have a responsibility to the group as a whole.

By establishing a fair and consistent health policy, you are demonstrating to all the parents that you know how to care for their children. And just as trust is an important part of your relationship with the children, it is also crucial that you form a trusting and respectful relationship with their parents.

The following illness policies will provide a framework to determine when children are too sick to be in your home. Unless your program has special facilities for caring for children with infectious illnesses, the American Academy of Pediatrics recommends that you exclude children who have the following symptoms or illnesses:

- fever (particularly if over 101°)
- diarrhea (especially if accompanied by another symptom such as fever or vomiting or if there are two or more cases among the children, their families, or the staff)
- vomiting (especially if accompanied by another symptom)
- chickenpox
- measles and rubella
- mumps
- tuberculosis
- whooping cough
- hepatitis
- being too sick to participate

In addition, certain rashes, until diagnosed, may be grounds for exclusion and children with symptoms of pinkeye should be excluded until diagnosed and treated.

- Do not accept medicine from a parent unless it is properly labeled with the child's name, the correct dosage, the name of the pharmacy to be contacted if questions arise, and the name and phone number of the prescribing doctor.

- You should have emergency information for each child in your home. Many caregivers keep index cards which include the child's full name, birthdate, and any food or drug allergies. It also should include the names and phone numbers of the parents, and the child's physician who can be contacted in case of an emergency. Additional information caregivers include is the parent's authorization for you to seek emergency care at a local hospital or clinic, and names of other adults who are authorized to pick up the child from your home.

An important focus of your attention as caregiver is to be alert and observant of changes in the child's health. These symptoms may first appear to you in subtle form. It is advisable to record the changes and verify whether they repeat, intensify or (hopefully) disappear during the course of the day.

When you communicate your observations to the parents you reinforce the partnership and shared responsibility for the child's health. Feel free to call them at work if the symptoms worsen.

Additional signs of illness to be noted are:

- Fatigue, lethargy
- Irritability, extended crying
- Loss of appetite
- Complaints of pain
- Itching and rashes

The following chart of common illnesses is intended to serve as a guide to help you recognize signs of infection. Please share this chart with parents. The child's doctor should be called if indicated.

CHILDHOOD ILLNESS CHART

	SYMPTOMS	INCUBATION/ DURATION
BRONCHITIS	Frequent coughing. Labored breathing. Possible fever.	1 to 7 days; 2 to 4 days.
CHICKEN POX	Fever. Discomfort. Itching. Pink or red spots on the chest, stomach and back, which may spread to the scalp and face. Spots change to blisters, which eventually crust.	10 to 21 days; 7 to 10 days.
COMMON COLD	Sneezing. Stuffed or runny nose. Sore throat. Watery eyes. Possible cough, chills, low fever.	1 to 7 days; 2 to 14 days.
CROUP	Labored breathing. Hoarseness. Loud hacking cough. Often comes on at night.	2 to 6 days; 4 to 5 days.
GERMAN MEASLES (RUBELLA)	Chills. Low fever (sometimes high). Runny nose. Painful swelling of glands behind the ears. Usually there is a slightly raised fine red rash, which begins on the face, then spreads over the entire body.	14 to 21 days; 3 to 6 days.
INFLUENZA (VIRUS, FLU)	Chills. Drowsiness. Weakness. Sudden high fever. Headache. Achiness. Sore throat. No appetite. Possible nausea and dizziness.	1 to 3 days; 3 to 7 days.
MEASLES	Early symptoms include low fever, slight hacking cough, fatigue, discomfort, eye irritation. Around the 4th day, fever and cough worsen and a rash of faint pink spots appears on the neck and cheeks, then spreads to the rest of the body.	10 to 15 days; 8 to 12 days.
MUMPS	Swollen glands on one or both sides of the jaw. Mild headache. Fever.	12 to 24 days; 6 to 10 days.
PNEUMONIA	Coughing. Fever. Rapid breathing. Discomfort. Chills. Weakness. Possible nausea and vomiting. Sudden fever lasting several days.	2 to 14 days; About 7 days.
ROSEOLA	Sudden fever lasting several days. After fever is gone, a rash of flat or raised spots appears on the chest, stomach or back, then spreads to the rest of the body.	10 to 14 days; 5 to 6 days.
SCARLET FEVER	Painful sore throat. Fever. Nausea and vomiting. Within 3 days a fine rash appears on the neck, armpit and groin, then spreads over the body.	1 to 5 days; 6 to 8 days.
STREP THROAT	Painful sore throat. Fever. Nausea and vomiting.	2 to 5 days; About 6 days.

VOMITING AND DIARRHEA

Consult your doctor if vomiting or diarrhea persists for more than 6 hours, contains blood or is accompanied by high fever. Have the child rest and keep him off solid foods. When he starts to feel better, give him low fat foods and frequent small amounts of liquid.

TREATMENT	CONTAGIOUSNESS
Consult your doctor. If the child has fever, make sure he rests, give him plenty of juice and use a vaporizer.	2 days before symptoms appear to 2 days after.
Consult your doctor. Rest is essential. Relieve itching with calamine lotion. Trim the child's nails so he doesn't scratch himself. Keep his utensils and dishes separate.	1 day before spots appear to about 6 days after. The child should be isolated until blisters crust and dry.
If the child has fever, make sure he rests, give him plenty of juice and use a vaporizer. Keep him warm and avoid chilling. Consult your doctor if the symptoms persist or worsen.	2 days before symptoms appear to 2 days after.
Consult your doctor. Use a vaporizer. Keep the child on a light, low fat diet.	2 days before symptoms appear to 5 days after.
If the child has fever, make sure he rests, give him plenty of juice and use a vaporizer. Keep the child's hands clean. Launder his linen and clothes separately.	7 days before symptoms appear to 5 days after. **Pregnant women should never be exposed to this illness.**
Consult your doctor. If the child has fever, make sure he rests, give him plenty of juice and use a vaporizer. Keep his utensils and dishes separate.	1 day before symptoms appear to 7 days after.
Consult your doctor. If the child's eyes are sensitive to light, keep the room dim. If he has fever, make sure he rests, give him plenty of juice and use a vaporizer. Keep his utensils and dishes separate.	4 days before rash appears to 5 days after.
Consult your doctor. Rest is essential. Apply cool compresses to the cheeks. **Do not** give the child citrus juices. Keep his utensils and dishes separate.	7 days before symptoms appear to 9 days after.
Consult your doctor. Make sure the child rests. Give him plenty of juice. Use a vaporizer. Keep him on a light, low fat diet.	Varies
Consult your doctor.	Varies
Consult your doctor. Make sure the child rests. Give him plenty of fluids. Check other family members for symptoms.	1 day before symptoms appear to 6 days after.
Consult your doctor. If the child has fever, make sure he rests and give him plenty of juice. Check other family members for symptoms.	1 day before symptoms appear to 6 days after.

TO NOURISH / TO NURTURE

Satisfying children's basic need to be fed when they are hungry is another step in forming loving and trusting relationships with children. Providing nutritious food in a relaxed and accepting atmosphere encourages good eating habits which can last a lifetime.

Mealtime is a child's first social experience. Whether offered the breast or a bottle, the baby has an opportunity to communicate her needs to another person. As children grow, they build upon their mealtime experiences. Toddlers enjoy joining the group at the table. They watch and learn as the older children eat and talk about the day.

Your involvement in mealtime can turn this daily occurrence into an enriched learning experience. Section III examined some of the ways caregiving routines are influenced by a child's development. This section discusses the importance of feeding as a time to nourish children's sense of self, as well as to nourish their bodies.

Think about ways you can structure mealtime routines.

(1) Meals and snacks served at approximately the same time each day help to build a pattern or routine into your day. When children can anticipate, or predict, when meals and snacks will be served, they begin to feel a sense of security. They can trust that their needs will be met.

(2) By being involved and participating in the children's mealtime, you give them a model for manners and appropriate mealtime behaviors. They look to you for examples...how to hold a spoon or drink from a cup. Your quiet tone of voice and relaxed and friendly attitude help the children to relax and talk quietly to each other.

(3) Eating is a sensory experience. Encourage the children to taste, smell and touch the food. By offering choices between a variety of nutritious foods, you can give children an opportunity to make decisions and feel a sense of autonomy.

"Would you like the tortillas first, or the beans?"
"May I offer you some fruit to eat with your sandwich?"

Offering choices is also one way to build more advanced intellectual concepts into your program. *"Do you prefer the orange cheese or the white cheese? The square cracker or the round one? Do you want two pieces or three?"*

GUIDELINES FOR ENJOYING MEALTIME

- A healthy child who feels well and is hungry will usually eat.
  - Encourage children to try new foods.
  - Respect individual food preferences.

  - Serve food that looks appetizing and attractive.
  - Praise children for good eating habits.

  - Remember that children's appetites vary from time to time.
  - Children like food they can eat with their fingers.

  - Visit with the children and encourage them to talk with each other.
  - Don't rush. Take your time and enjoy the relaxed atmosphere.

  - Make hand washing a crucial part of your mealtime routine.
  - Try not to add sugar or salt to the children's food.

- Be aware of, and post in your kitchen, the food allergies of children in your care.
- Let the baby's parents set the pace for introducing solids and new foods. They will appreciate your observations and feedback.
- Inform parents when you have served new foods to their children.
- Do not give babies raw carrots, nuts or seeds unless mashed or finely shredded. Avoid all small hard foods, such as popcorn, that can choke the baby.

The USDA Child and Adult Food Program (CACFP) reimburses caregivers for the meals and snacks served to the children. Contact your local child care resource and referral agency, licensing or registration office or family daycare association for more information about CACFP.

FOUR BASIC FOOD GROUPS

Milk Group: milk, yogurt, cheese	Bread Group: Bread and Cereals, noodles, rice, grains, grits and tortillas
Protein Group: Meat, fish, poultry, eggs, cottage cheese, peas, beans, nuts and peanut butter	Fruit and Vegetables include dark green or yellow vegetables, juices, melons, potatoes

Chapter 13

A WORD ABOUT CHILD ABUSE

As caregivers you are also in the position to observe parenting styles which do not feel comfortable to you. You may observe a parent being too rough or too menacing with a child. You may witness or hear about punishments which seem unusually harsh and inappropriate.

Your role in these cases is twofold: First, you must assess the situation in terms of what you know to be in the best interest of children. Secondly, you must consider your own legal and moral responsibilities. Child Abuse Reporting Laws are intended to protect children and to protect you from being unjustly accused of abuse while you are caring for children in you home. It is easy for parents who are too rough with their children to point to you, unless you follow the laws designed to protect the children in your care.

Family day care providers as child care professionals who are in daily contact with children should report abusive incidents when they are observed or if there is reasonable suspicion. A telephone report to a child protective agency should be made immediately upon suspicion or knowledge. Report the following: physical abuse, sexual abuse, severe or general neglect, willful cruelty or unjustifiable punishment of a child, cruel and inhumane corporal punishment, unjustifiable mental suffering.

Child abuse reporting laws were designed to protect the child and to get help for the family. For updated information or to make a report you may call the Child Abuse Hotline, 1-800-422-4453. Check your state regulations with regard to reporting procedures and specific state laws.

Make clear to parents that you report suspected child abuse during your orientation and contract process. Your clarity early in the relationship will reassure them. Also tell the parents that you will be teaching their children to say "no" if someone touches their private parts. Children must be taught that if anyone touches them in a way that makes them feel uncomfortable, this should be reported to an adult.

The following chart from the S.F. Child Abuse Council describes some of the typical responses of children to abuse. They may exhibit symptoms at different developmental stages. These responses overlap and are not designed to be rigidly applied. They are general guidelines. All children respond to abuse individually.

	PHYSICAL ABUSE	SEXUAL ABUSE	NEGLECT
INFANT/TODDLERS	Withdrawal/Apathy Aggressive behavior Head-banging Hypervigilance Fearfulness/Anxiety Subdued crying Clinginess Poor eye contact Indiscriminant attaching Extreme or inappropriate reactions to pain	Sexualized behavior (Excessive masturbation or inserting objects) Stiff body/difficulty sleeping, relaxing Clingy Difficulty eating Colicky Passive/withdrawn Fussy	Withdrawal/Apathy Rocking Fearfulness Lethargic
PRESCHOOLERS/SCHOOL-AGE	Withdrawal/Apathy Aggressive behavior Self-destructive behavior Attention-getting (e.g. fire setting) Self-mutilation/accident prone School difficulties Speech or learning difficulties Fear of failure Drug or alcohol abuses Running away	Sexualized behavior Inability to relate to peers Seeks out or avoids adults Parentified (pseudo-mature) Manipulative behavior Distracted easily/daydreams Self-conscious behavior Eating disorders (bulimia, obesity, anorexia) School problems	Withdrawal/Apathy Fearful Learned Helplessness (can't reach out for help) Hordes food Clingy or needy Pseudo-independent Regressive behavior (thumb-sucking, head banging)
ADOLESCENTS	Withdrawal/Apathy Aggressive Behavior Anti-social Behavior (e.g. car theft, truancy) Inability to relate to peers Identifies with "tough guy" image (punk-rock, gangs) Seeks out attention of adults Prostitution Running away Drug and alcohol abuse Eating/school problems	Sexualized behavior and acting out Promiscuity/Prostitution Defiance or compliance to extreme Isolated Fearful/anxious Self-mutilating Suicidal gestures Obsessively clean Pseudo-mature Eating disorders Drug and alcohol abuse Delinquent behavior/running away	Withdrawal/Apathy Aggressiveness Obesity or other eating disorder Inability to make or keep friends Unkempt to extreme Drug and alcohol abuse
ADULTS	Inability to form longlasting, meaningful, or satisfying relationships Ends up in violent situations Isolated Frequent relocations Extremely angry or fearful Low Self-esteem	Sexual difficulties (physical problems or intimacy issues) Distrust Shame of body Sees value only in sexuality Unable to assert/protect self Feels victimized Drug/alcohol abuse Low self-esteem	Relationship difficulties Depression Alcoholism/drug abuse Isolated Lack of interest in self or others

Chapter 14
DECIDING TO OPEN YOUR FAMILY DAY CARE HOME

STATE REGULATIONS FOR FAMILY DAY CARE:

There are 224,000 regulated providers nationwide (*1990 Family Day Care Licensing Study, The Children's Foundation*). Your state may require you to obtain a license or registration certificate to operate a family day care home. A complete list of Family Day Care State Regulatory Agencies can be found on page 116, which will help you identify what your state requires.

As consumers of child care, parents are aware that a license or registration certificate is no guarantee of quality. They realize that many factors, like affordability and location, will influence their child care decision.

How you present yourself and your program will influence your success at recruiting and keeping clients. Your license or registration will indicate that you have fulfilled the requirements and are willing to comply and adhere to regulations intended to monitor child care.

This book has offered hundreds of ways you can enhance your home environment and relationships with children. Most of these suggestions offer a way you can care for children while they are growing up.

Your ability to form relationships which encourage a sense of specialness and uniqueness with children and their families is your best measure of success.

As a regulated caregiver you have responsibilities to the children, the families and to your community. You also have an obligation to society as a whole to protect and safeguard the children in your care.

Although you are not their parent, you do have a partnership with their families. You are often in the position to see and hear things about how the children are being raised.

This information can be very valuable to you. You need to ask if children have had a good night's sleep; and their parents need to know how much lunch they ate and how long they slept at nap time.

Although you are not their parent, you do have a partnership with their families. You are often in the position to see and hear things about how the children are being raised.

This information can be very valuable to you. You need to ask if children have had a good night's sleep; and their parents need to know how much lunch they ate and how long they slept at nap time.

Parents choose a family day care home setting as an alternative to center-based care because they are attracted to the personalized and individualized style of caring for children. They may appreciate this intimacy and often form mutually supportive relationships with you.

In an era when single parent families are increasing and contact with the extended family is more difficult, you may find that parents turn to you more and more for guidance and child care advice.

Know yourself and your limits. You are the best person to determine your own suitability to work with young children on a daily basis. You may want to answer the following questions as a method of assessing your own motives.

- Are you energetic and healthy?
- Do you like to have children around?
- Do you enjoy playing with them?
- Do you enjoy being at home?
- Are you resourceful?
- Are you flexible? Do you have a sense of humor?
- Do you enjoy talking to parents?
- Do you feel committed to children and their families?

If you have answered yes to most of these questions and feel you have the support of your family and neighbors, you are in an ideal position to establish a child care program in your home. Before you begin, there are some considerations:

- What ages do you want to take into your care?

  - In some states the ages and numbers served are limited by licensing regulations, so check these restrictions and adhere to them.

- Decide what hours you want to be open.

  - Determine a policy for those families who request overtime or extended care.

- Will you take children with special needs?

- Children with special needs are more like others than they are different. They need to be encouraged to help themselves as much as possible, and the small size and personalized care that your program offers may be the optimal setting. Children with special needs learn through the same kinds of experiences as other children learn, so as a caregiver you already know many ways to work with these children.

- Have you consulted your own family and neighbors on their feelings about your home being a family day care home?

- Have you discussed problems like increased street traffic, and family dinnertime after a late pick-up? Everyone's support and cooperation can make a big difference at the end of the day when you are tired, the house is a mess, and your own children (or spouse) are demanding a little quality time too.

- Are you prepared to run a small business?

- Family day care is a business, and the families you serve are the clients. Be prepared to enter into a contractual agreement which details your mutual expectations about: hours, fees, vacations, meals, illness, etc. Sample contracts are included in this chapter. Determine which works best for you or write your own.

- Understand that as a proprietor of a small business you are expected to keep accurate records.

- Some caregivers find it easiest to keep a separate checking account for their family day care home. This way fees, payments and expenses are recorded for income tax purposes (Schedule C of Form 1040, Profit/Loss From Business).

- You may want to consult an accountant for help in setting up your records. For complete information about the financial end of your business, consult *Basic Guide to Family Day Care Record Keeping* published by Toys 'n Things Press, St. Paul, Minnesota.

- You will also want to have liability insurance, which can be difficult to obtain and costly. Your homeowners policy will not cover your business. For information on insurance options, consult your local child care resource and referral agency or your local family day care association, or the National Association for Family Day Care 202-347-3356.

This series of steps and regulations may seem complicated. The criteria for regulation, however, were designed to establish standards of quality care for children outside of their own homes. Compliance with laws does not guarantee safety. Parents are the consumers of child care, and they are becoming increasingly more suspicious of caregivers who work alone with children all day. Their concerns are valid, and there are things you can do to put them at ease.

(1) Invite them to visit your program unannounced. They should know that their children are accessible to them at any time. Abuse happens in programs where parents are told to keep restricted hours (so the program won't be interrupted).

(2) Make sure parents feel comfortable to be in any part of your home where you are caring for children. Parents worry that "back rooms" are places where children can be molested. The notion of dropping off children at the gate, although convenient for you, also makes you a target for parental worries. Children should be taken in and out of the door by a responsible adult.

(3) Share the telephone numbers of other families using your home. Parents who can talk to each other about the good job you are doing can be a wonderful support system for each other and for you. Parents shopping for a new care situation for their child should also be able to talk to one or two of your clients for reference.

(4) One of the most common problems among family day care providers is misunderstandings with parents. A clear agreement at the start of the child care relationship can reduce or prevent many misunderstandings. This is one of the important reasons to use provider-parent contracts. The other crucial reason is to give you a basis for suing (or threatening to sue) if the parent refuses to pay or breaks another important part of the contract. Parents expect you to treat their children with respect. You have the right to expect parents to treat you with respect as the professional caregiver you are.

(5) To make sure that both the parents and the provider understand the rules and regulations of the family day care home, the provider should have a "policy statement" in addition to the contract. This will help to avoid misunderstandings later on.

FAMILY CHILD CARE AGREEMENT FORM

1. Childcare is provided _______ through _______ during parents working hours.
2. Childcare fees are based on a five-day week, including holidays and absence from illness, and must be paid in full.
3. Pay day will be every __________________ upon departure.
4. Parents are required to notify the Day Care Home two full weeks in advance when child is to be withdrawn to accompany parents on summer vacation. Parents then will be required to pay ½ the regular week rate, IN ADVANCE for the vacation time in order to insure readmission.
5. CHRISTMAS VACATION ½ pay of regular week rate.
6. Two week notice is required before removing child from this home or two weeks pay. (THIS MAY BE PRORATED)
7. Notify our home by phone by _________ if child is not coming for the day.
8. Must bring Infant Formula and/or special food for child.
9. Please no candy, gum, or money, and no toys.
10. Celery, fruit, cookies, etc. are fine, but please bring enough for all.
11. Please bring plenty of disposable diapers and a change of clothing.
12. Give prompt notice of change in address or telephone numbers at home or work or medical insurance plans.
13. Children must be dressed, and ready to begin the day.
14. List any known or suspected allergies (food, medication, etc.) or special medical problems. Medications must have child's name on label.
15. All children must have their immunizations within 30 days after placement in this home.
16. Reimbursement for any damages of $10 or more while child is in this home will be expected.
17. I give my permission for __________________________ to travel by car whenever necessary, while in this daycare home, with appropriate car seat restraints as required by the State of California.
18. I will pick up ________________ promptly by ________________ each day.
19. I agree to pay $ PER WEEK for child care for _____________. OVERTIME WILL BE $3.00 EXTRA. Care provided for child _________ minutes after normal pickup time will be considered overtime.

I __________________________________ AGREE TO ALL OF THE ABOVE.

DAY CARE PROVIDER SIGNATURE ______________________________ DATE ________

PARENT SIGNATURE _______________________________________ DATE ________

PROVIDER DUPLICATE—PARENT ORIGINAL
SAMPLE

CONCLUSION

Operating a family day care home can be both rewarding and challenging. How you structure your hours, fees and program will influence your life and the lives of the families you serve. This book has attempted to offer a range of ideas which you can apply to your own personal style of caring for children.

Remember that adults as well as children have their own personal and individual style. The way you interact with your own family and friends is often the way you enjoy working with the families you serve.

Many caregivers feel that their family day care business is a part of their extended family. With some families there is an easy rapport and mutual respect which enables these relationships to grow into long lasting friendships. Other families seem demanding and inflexible, while still others seem satisfied but not really involved in the day to day routine of your program.

As the proprietor of a small business you have the right to select clients who seem to "match" your style of caring for children. In fact, you have probably already noticed that you develop better working relationships with parents who share similar views on issues such as discipline, nutrition and health.

These adult relationships are also very important for the children. One concern, as increasing numbers of women with children under two (56%) enter the workforce, is the number of childcare situations the children experience during their first six years.

As caregivers, you can help parents choose a childcare placement for their child which will last for a prolonged period of time. By pointing out how your "style" of child-caring is similar to theirs, you help parents choose a setting which will work best for the child. Some caregivers schedule "parent meetings" a couple of times during the year, so parents have the opportunity to get together to share their experiences and hear from you about your program.

Parent satisfaction and continued enrollment in the program are key to stability for both your program and the children you serve. By providing consistent and stable environments for children and their families you are providing a model for future relationships.

Your commitment to children and their families today will affect their future growth and well-being. You have chosen a difficult and challenging career. Good luck and best wishes with your family day care program.

REFERENCES

ACCIDENT PREVENTION AND FIRST AID

American Medical Association. *Handbook of First Aid and Emergency Care.* New York: Random House, 1980.

American National Red Cross. *Standard First Aid and Personal Safety.* Garden City, NY: Doubleday, 1973.

Green, M. *A Sigh of Relief—The First Aid Handbook for Childhood Emergencies.* New York, Bantam Books, 1977.

Sharlatt, E., ed. *Kids Day In and Day Out.* New York: Simon & Schuster, 1979.

Telephone Directory, "Survival Guide", Front Section of Telephone Directories, 1985.

IN SICKNESS AND IN HEALTH

Allison, L. *Blood and Guts—A Working Guide to Your Insides.* Boston, MA: Little Brown & Co., 1975.

Black, H., ed. *The Berkeley Co-op Food Book.* Palo Alto, CA: Bull Publishing, 1980.

Burns, M. *Good for Me! All About Food in 32 Bites.* Covela CA: Yolla Bolly Press, 1978.

Feinbloom, R., M.D. and Boston Children's Medical Center. *The Complete Guide for Parents.* New York: Dell Publishing Co., 1975.

Lunsky, V. *Feed Me, I'm Yours.* New York: Bantam Books, 1977.

Parents Nursery School. *Kids Are Natural Cooks.* Boston, MA: Houghton Mifflin, 1974.

Samuels, M. M.D., and Samuels, N. *The Well Baby.* New York: Summit, 1979.

Schiller, J., M.D. *Childhood Illness—A Common Sense Approach.* New York: Stein and Day, 1974.

Stein, S. *The Kids Kitchen Takeover.* New York: Perigee Books, 1981.

Vaughn, G. *A Pictorial Guide to Common Childhood Illnesses.* London: Berkeley Graphics, Ltd., 1970.

CHILD ABUSE

Corcoran, Clodagh. *Take Care!: Preventing Child Sexual Abuse*. Chester Springs, PA: Dufour Editions, 1987.

Jorgenson, E. Clay. *Child Abuse: A Practical Guide for Those Who Help Others.* New York: Crossroads/Continuum 1990.

Mufson, Susan & Kranz, Rachel. *Straight Talk About Child Abuse.* New York: Facts on File. 1991.

Sabatino, David A. *Fine Line: When Discipline Becomes Child Abuse.* New York: Blue Ridge Summit, PA: TAB Books, 1991.

Tower, Cynthia C. Secret Scars: A Guide for Survivors of Child Sexual Abuse. New York: Penguin USA, 1989.

DECIDING TO OPEN YOUR FAMILY DAY CARE HOME

1990 Family Day Care Licensing Study, The Children's Foundation, 725 Fifteenth Street, N.W. #505, Washington, D.C. 20005.

Harms, T., Clifford, R. and Radan-Belking, E. *The Day Care Home Environment Rating Scale*. N.Y. Teachers College Press, 1980.

——. *Early Childhood Environment Rating Scale*. North Carolina. Teachers College Press, 1980.

——. Homebased Day Care Training Program. Developed for the Day Care Section, North Carolina Department of Human Resources. University of North Carolina at Chapel Hill. 1981.

Learning With Joy, Inc., America's Children Multicultural Series, P.O. Box 32237, San Jose, CA 95152.

Mrs. Greene's Kapers For Kids, Curriculum and Crafts Kits. 5340 Calvin Avenue, Tarzana, CA 91356.

National Association for Family Day Care, 725 Fifteenth Street, N.W. Suite 505, Washington, D.C. 20005.

Resources For Family Day Care Providers. Toys 'n Things Press, 450 N. Syndicate, #5, St. Paul, MN 55104.

STATE BY STATE LIST OF REGULATORY AGENCIES

[Reprinted with permission from the *1990 Family Day Care Licensing Study*, The Children's Foundation, Washington, DC]

ALABAMA
Ms. June Perry, Supervisor
Dept. of Human Resources
Office of Day Care and Child Development
50 Ripley St.
Montgomery, AL 36130
(205) 242-1425

ALASKA
Patricia O'Brien
Dept. of Health & Social Services
Family and Youth Services
Box H-05-0630
Juneau, AK 99811
(907) 465-2145

ARIZONA
Sue Prete
Dept. of Economic Security
Administration for Children, Youth and Families
P.O. Box 6123
Phoenix, AZ 85005
(602) 542-2360

ARKANSAS
Kathy Stegall
Division of Children and Family Services
P.O. Box 1437 Slot 720
Little Rock, AR 72203
(501) 682-8590

CALIFORNIA
Pat Flahavan
Dept. of Social Services
Community Care Licensing Division
Central Operations Branch
744 P Street, M.S. 19-50
Sacramento, CA 95814
(916) 324-4303

COLORADO
Grace Hardy
Office of Child Care Services
Dept. of Social Services
1575 Sherman Street
Denver, CO 80203-1714
(303) 866-5958

CONNECTICUT
Richard Charnick
Dept. of Human Resources
Day Care
1049 Asylum Avenue
Hartford, CT 06105-2431
(203) 566-3800

DELAWARE
Pauline D. Koch
Office of Child Care Licensing
Department of Services for Children, Youth, and Their Families
1825 Faulkland Road
Wilmington, DE 19805-1195
(302) 633-2700, 633-2670

DISTRICT OF COLUMBIA
Angela Hayes
Department of Consumer and Regulatory Affairs
Service Facility, Regulations Administration
614 H St., N.W., Room 1014
Washington, D.C. 20001
(202) 727-7226

FLORIDA
Pamela Hutchison
Dept. of Health and Rehabilitation Services
Children, Youth & Families Program Office
1317 Winewood Blvd., Building 8, Room 320
Tallahassee, FL 32301
(904) 488-4900

GEORGIA
Marsh A. Gates
Child Care Licensing
878 Peachtree St., NE, Room 607
Atlanta, GA 30309
(404) 894-5688

HAWAII
Carol Chang
Dept. of Human Services
P.O. Box 339
Honolulu, HI 96809
(808) 548-2302

IDAHO
Perry Ackerman
Dept. of Health and Welfare
450 West State Street
Boise, ID 83720
(208) 334-5702

ILLINOIS
Thomas Felder
Licensing Specialist
Dept. of Children and Family Services
406 East Monroe Street
Springfield, IL 62701-1498
(217) 785-2592

INDIANA
Keith Carver, Supervisor
Day Care Licensing Unit
Dept. of Public Welfare
141 S. Meridian St., 6th Fl.
Indianapolis, IN 46225
(317) 232-4442

IOWA
Don Kassar
Dept. of Human Services
Hoover State Office Building, 5th Fl.
Des Moines, IA 50319
(515) 281-6074, 281-3186

KANSAS
Shirley Norris
Department of Health and Environment
900 S.W. Jackson
Landon State Office Bldg.
Topeka, KS 66612-1290
(913) 296-1272

KENTUCKY
Bess Howard
Human Services Program Specialist
Licensing and Regulation
275 East Main Street
CHR Building, 4th Floor, East
Frankfort, KY 40621
(502) 564-2800

LOUISIANA
Mary Tauzin
Day Care Home Admin.
Department of Education
P.O. Box 94064
Baton Rouge, LA 70804-9064
(504) 342-3707

MAINE
James R. Floyd
Dept. of Human Services
Child Care Licensing Unit
State House Station 11
Augusta, ME 04333
(207) 289-5060

MARYLAND
Regina Bernard
Office of Child Care Licensing and Regulation
Community College of Baltimore
600 E. Lombard St., Rm. 312
Baltimore, MD 21202
(301) 333-0193

MASSACHUSETTS
Martha J. Roberts
Day Care Director
Office for Children
10 West St., 5th Floor
Boston, MA 02111
(617) 727-8900

MICHIGAN
Ted de Wolf, Director
Dept. of Social Services
Child Day Care Licensing
235 S. Grand Ave., Suite 1212
Lansing, MI 48909
(517) 373-8300

MINNESOTA
James Loving, Director
Licensing Division
Dept. of Human Services
444 Lafayette Rd.
St. Paul, MN 55155-3842
(612) 296-3971

MISSISSIPPI
Diane Herring
Child Care Licensing Dir.
State Board of Health
P.O. Box 1700
Jackson, MS 39215-1700
(601) 960-7504, (800) 227-6880

MISSOURI
Pat Wojciehowski
Child Care Licensing Unit
Division of Family Services
P.O. Box 88
Jefferson City, MO 65103
(314) 751-2450

MONTANA
Charles McCarthy
Dept. of Family Services
P.O. Box 8005
Helena, MT 59604
(406) 444-5900

NEBRASKA
Deb Dawson
Dept. of Social Services
P.O. Box 95026
Lincoln, NE 68509
(402) 471-9132

NEVADA
Patricia J. Hedgecoth, Chief
Child Care Services
505 E. King St., Room 101
Carson City, NV 89710
(702) 687-5911

NEW HAMPSHIRE
Robert Letellier
Bureau of Child Care, Standards and Licensing
Health & Human Svcs. Bldg.
6 Hazen Drive
Concord, NH 03301-6527
(603) 271-4624

NEW JERSEY
Richard Crane, Acting Chief
Bureau of Licensing
CN 717
Trenton, NJ 08625
(609) 292-9220

NEW MEXICO
Stephen M. Borland
Licensing and Certification Bureau
1190 St. Francis Dr., Runnel's Bldg.
Santa Fe, NM 87503
(505) 827-2444

NEW YORK STATE
Joseph Capo
Bureau of Child Care
New York State Department of Social Services
40 N. Pearl Street, 11-B
Albany, NY 12243
(518) 474-5926

NEW YORK CITY
Agency for Child Development
240 Church St.
New York, NY 10013
(212) 553-6288

NEW YORK CITY
Department of Health
Bureau of Day Care
65 Worth St.
New York, NY 10013

NORTH CAROLINA
Bebie Cole
Division of Facility Services
Child Day Care Section
701 Barbour Drive
Raleigh, NC 27603
(919) 733-4801

NORTH DAKOTA
Paul Ronningen
Office of Human Services
State Capital Building
Bismarck, ND 58501
(701) 224-4809

OHIO
M. Pauline Hosenfeld, Chief
Child Care Services
Dept. of Human Services
30 E. Broad St., 30th Floor
Columbus, OH 43215
(614) 466-3822

OKLAHOMA
Nancy von Bargen
Dept. of Human Services
P.O. Box 25352
Oklahoma City, OK 73125
(405) 521-3561

OREGON
Karen Moffat
Day Care Unit
198 Commercial St., S.E.
Salem, OR 97310
(503) 378-3178, AC 503

PENNSYLVANIA
Susan Miller
Day Care Division
Office of Children, Youth and Families
Dept. of Public Welfare
Complex 3, 4th Floor
P.O. Box 2675
Harrisburg, PA 17105
(717) 787-1529

RHODE ISLAND
JoAnne K. Flodin
Department for Children and Their Families
Community Services and Day Care Licensing
610 Mt. Pleasant Ave.
Providence, RI 02908
(401) 457-4995

SOUTH CAROLINA
Helen Baxter and Barbara Yandle
Office of Children and Family Services
Dept. of Social Services
P.O. Box 1520
Columbia, SC 29202
(803) 734-5740

SOUTH DAKOTA
David Hanson
Dept. of Social Services
Child Protection Division
Kneip Building
700 Governors Dr.
Pierre, SD 57501
(605) 773-3227

TENNESSEE
Carolyn Deal
Licensing Unit
Dept. of Human Services
Citizens Plaza
400 Deaderick
Nashville, TN 37219
(615) 741-7129

TEXAS
T. Douglas Sanders
Dept. of Human Services
P.O. Box 149030
Mail Code 550-W
Austin, TX 78714-9030
(512) 450-3253

UTAH
Carmen E. Cintron
Dept. of Social Services
Office of Licensing
120 North 200 West
Salt Lake City, UT 84114
(801) 538-4003

VERMONT
Coleman Baker
Children's Day Care Unit
Licensing and Registration
103 S. Main St.
Waterbury, VT 05676
(802) 241-2158

VIRGINIA
Elizabeth Campbell
Division of Licensing
8007 Discovery Drive
Richmond, VA 23228
(804) 662-9025

WASHINGTON
Barry Fibel, Licensing Specialist
Division of Children and Family Services
Mail Stop-OB-41
Olympia, WA 98504
(206) 753-0204

WEST VIRGINIA
Kay Tilton
Dept. of Human Services
1900 Washington St., East
Capitol Complex, Bldg.6, Room 850-B
Charleston, WV 25305
(304) 348-7980

WISCONSIN
David B. Edie
Dept. of Health and Social Services
Bureau for Children, Youth and Families
P.O. Box 7851
Madison, WI 53707
(608) 266-8200

WYOMING
Ken Kaz
Division of Public Assistance
Hathaway Building
Cheyenne, WY 82002-0710
(307) 777-5994

HOME CENTERED CARE BIBLIOGRAPHY

Arns, Betsy. *The Survival Guide to School-Age Child Care*. Huntington Beach, CA: School-Age Workshops Press, 1988.

Bergstrom, Joan M. *School's Out.* Berkeley, CA: Ten Speed Press, 1990.

Brown, Sam Ed. *Bubbles, Rainbows & Worms: Science Experiments for Pre-School Children*. Mt. Rainier, MD: Gryphon House, Inc., 1981.

Colgin, Mary Lou, comp. *One Potato, Two Potato, Three Potato, Four: 165 Chants for Children.* Mt. Rainier, MD: Gryphon House, Inc., 1982. Previously published as *Chants for Children*.

Collins, Alice H., and Eunice L. Watson. *Family Day Care: A Practical Guide for Parents, Caregivers, & Professionals.* Boston, MA: Beacon Press, 1976.

Connolly, Ann Marie, and Helen Gibson, eds. and comps. *Rainy Day Activities for Preschoolers.* Mercer Island, WA: Mercer Island Preschool Association, 1988. Distributed by Gryphon House, Inc.

Copeland, Tom. *Basic Guide to Family Day Care Record Keeping*. Family Day Care Business Series. St. Paul, MN: Toys 'n Things, 1988. Distributed by Gryphon House, Inc.

Copeland, Tom. *Family Day Care Tax Workbook*, 1989. Family Day Care Business Series. St. Paul, MN: Toys 'n Things, 1989.

Cromwell, Liz, Dixie Hibner, and John R. Faitel, comps. *Finger Frolics*. Livonia, MI: Partner Press, 1976. rev. ed., 1983. Distributed by Gryphon House, Inc.

Crone, J. Edwin. *Getting Started as a Residential Child Care Worker? A Guide for Beginners*. Washington, DC: Child Welfare, 1983.

Denis, Terri. *A Daycare Mother's Manual: How to Start & Operate a Childcare Service in Your Home.* San Manuel, AZ: Fred Robot Factory, 1986.

Gallagher, Patricia. *Start Your Own At-Home Child Care Business.* New York: Doubleday, 1989.

Gellert, S., Hollestelle, K., and Kotlus, E. & The Equity Project Team; *Helping Children Love Themselves and Others: A Professional Handbook for Family Day Care*, Washington, DC: The Children's Foundation, 1990.

Gilbert, LaBritta. *Do Touch: Instant, Easy Hands-on Learning Experiences for Young Children.* Mt. Rainier, MD: Gryphon House, Inc., 1989.

Gilbert, LaBritta. *I Can Do It! I Can Do It! 135 Successful Independent Learning Activities*. Mt. Rainier, MD: Gryphon House, Inc., 1984.

Harms, Thelma, and Richard Clifford. *Family Day Care Rating Scale*. New York: Teachers College Press, 1989.

Honig, Alice S. *Playtime Learning Games for Young Children*. Syracuse, NY: Syracuse University Press, 1982.

Honig, Alice S., and J. Ronald Lally. *Infant Caregiving: A Design for Training*. Syracuse, NY: Syracuse University Press, 1981.

Hubbard, April, and Clementine Hayburn. *Day Care Parenting*. New York: Bart Books, 1988.

Jaisinghani, Vijay T., and Vivian G. Morris. *Child Care in a Family Setting: A Comprehensive Guide to Family Day Care*. Cheltenham, PA: Family Care Associates, 1986.

Johnson, Barbara. *Cup Cooking: Individual Child-Portion Picture Recipes*. Lake Alfred, FL: Early Educators Press, 1978. Distributed by Gryphon House, Inc.

Keith-Lucas, Alan, and Clifford W. Sanford. *Group Child Care as a Family Service*. Chapel Hill, NC: University of North Carolina Press, 1977.

Kohl, MaryAnn F. *Mudworks: Creative Clay, Dough, and Modeling Experiences*. Bellingham, WA: Bright Ring Publishing, 1989. Distributed by Gryphon House, Inc.

Lambert, Paul. *ABC's of Child Care Work in Residential Care*: The Linden Hill Manual. Washington, DC: Child Welfare, 1977.

Linderman, C. Emma. *Teachables from Trashables: Homemade Toys That Teach*. St. Paul, MN: Toys 'n Things Press, 1979. Distributed by Gryphon House, Inc.

McCrorey, Helen, and Dolores McCrorey. *The Business of Family Day Care*. Malibu, CA: Roundtable Publishing, Inc., 1988.

Miller, Karen. *Ages and Stages*. Chelsea, MA: Telshare Publishing Company, Inc., 1985. Distributed by Gryphon House, Inc.

Miller, Karen. *More Things to Do with Toddlers and Twos*. Chelsea, MA: Telshare Publishing Company, Inc., 1989. Distributed by Gryphon House, Inc.

Miller, Karen. *Things to Do with Toddlers and Twos*. Chelsea, MA: Telshare Publishing Company, Inc., 1984. Distributed by Gryphon House, Inc.

Modigliani, Kathy. *Opening Your Door to Children: How to Start a Family Day Care Program*. Washington, DC: National Association Child Ed., 1987.

Morgan, Gwen. *Alternatives for Regulation of Family Day Care Homes for Children*. Washington, DC: Day Care Council.

Moses, Kathy. *It's a Child's World: The Complete Guide to Day-Care; an Operational Manual for Providers, an Informational Guide for Parents*. Minot, ND: North American Heritage Press, 1989.

Müller, Brunhild. *Painting With Children*. First published in German under the title *Malen mit Wasserfarben*. Stuttgart: Verlag Freies Geistesleben, 1986. Translated by Donald Maclean. Edinburgh: Floris Books, 1987. Distributed by Gryphon House

Nelson, Eileen. *Calendar-Keeper, 1990: A Record Keeping System for Group Child Care Providers & Home Nursery Schools*. Family Day Care Business Series, 12th ed. St. Paul, MN: Toys 'n Things, 1989.

Nelson, Margaret K. *Negotiated Care: The Experience of Family Day Care Providers*. Philadelphia: Temple University Press, forthcoming.

Peters, Ellie R. *Home Child-Care: The Tender Business*. South Bend, IN: Greenlawn Press, 1990.

Pfeffer, Wendy. *Starting a Child Care Business, a Rewarding Career: A Home Study Course*. Home Study Series. Blawensburg NJ: Fruition Publications, 1989.

Powell, E. Sandy. *Heart to Heart Caregiving: A Sourcebook of Family Day Care Activities*, Projects & Practical Provider Support. St. Paul, MN: Toys 'n Things, 1990. Distributed by Gryphon House, Inc.

Prestine, Joan. *Family Day Care Activities A to Z*. Belmont, CA: David S. Lake Publishers, Fearon Teachers' Aids, 1989.

Provenzo, Jr., Eugene F., and Arlene Brett. *The Complete Block Book*. Syracuse, NY: Syracuse University Press, 1983. Distributed by Gryphon House, Inc.

Raines, Shirley C., and Robert J. Canady. *Story S-t-r-e-t-c-h-e-r-s: Activities to Expand Children's Favorite Books.* Mt. Rainier, MD: Gryphon House, Inc., 1989.

Redleaf, Rhoda. *Open the Door, Let's Explore: Neighborhood Field Trips for Young Children.* St. Paul, MN: Toys 'n Things Press, 1983. Distributed by Gryphon House, Inc.

Redleaf, Rhoda. *Teachables II: Homemade Toys that Teach.* St. Paul, MN: Toys 'n Things Press, 1987. Distributed by Gryphon House, Inc.

Rockwell, Robert E., Elizabeth A. Sherwood, and Robert A. Williams. *Hug a Tree: And Other Things to Do Outdoors with Young Children.* Mt. Rainier, MD: Gryphon House, Inc., 1986.

Roemer, Joan. *Two to Four from Nine to Five: The Adventures of a Day Care Provider*. New York: HarperCollins, 1989.

Saifer, Steffen. *Practical Solutions to Practically Every Problem: The Early Childhood Teacher's Manua*l. Foreword by Ellen Galinsky. St. Paul, MN: Toys 'n Things Press, 1990. Distributed by Gryphon House, Inc.

Schiller, Pam, and Joan Rossano. *The Instant Curriculum: 500 Developmentally Appropriate Learning Activities for Busy Teachers of Young Children.* Mt. Rainier, MD: Gryphon House, Inc., 1990.

Seltzer, M. Seligson, R. Kramer Baden, A. Genser, and James A. Levine. *School-Age Child Care: An Action Manual.* Westport, CT: Greenwood Press, Auburn House, 1982.

Sherwood, Elizabeth A., Robert A. Williams, and Robert E. Rockwell. *More Mudpies to Magnets: Science for Young Children.* Mt. Rainier, MD: Gryphon House, Inc., 1990.

Squibb, Betsy. *Family Day Care: How to Provide It in Your Home.* Boston: Harvard Common Press, 1980. rev. ed. 1986.

Stonehouse, Anne, ed. *Trusting Toddlers: Planning for One- to Three-Year-Olds in Child Care Centers.* Australian Early Childhood Association, Inc., 1988. Reprint. St. Paul, MN: Toys 'n Things Press, 1990. Distributed by Gryphon House, Inc.

Weissman, Jackie. *Games to Play with Babies.* Overland Park, KS: Miss Jackie Music Company, 1988. Distributed by Gryphon House, Inc.

Weissman, Jackie. *Songs to Sing with Babies.* Overland Park, KS: Miss Jackie Music Company, 1983. Distributed by Gryphon House, Inc.

Williams, Robert A., Robert E. Rockwell, and Elizabeth Sherwood. *Mudpies to Magnets: A Preschool Science Curriculum.* Mt. Rainier, MD: Gryphon House, Inc., 1987.

INDEX